Happiness and Other Small Things of Absolute Importance

Haim Shapira

Translated from the Hebrew by Baruch Gefen

WATKINS
Sharing Wisdom Since
1893

To my wife Daniela and my daughters Tal and Inbal

Haim Shapira was born in Lithuania in 1962. In 1977 he emigrated to Israel, where he earned a PhD in mathematical genetics for his dissertation on game theory and another PhD for his research on the mathematical and philosophical approaches to infinity. He now teaches mathematics, psychology, philosophy and literature. He is an author of seven bestselling books. His stated mission as a writer is not to try to make his readers agree with him, but simply to encourage them to enjoy thinking. One of Israel's most popular and sought-after speakers, he lectures on creativity and strategic thinking, existential philosophy and philosophy in children's literature, happiness and optimism, nonsense and insanity, imagination and the meaning of meaning, as well as friendship and love. He is also an accomplished pianist and an avid collector of anything beautiful.

From the same author:

Conversations on Game Theory
Infinity – The Neverending Story
Ecclesiastes, The Biblical Philosopher
Nocturnal Musings
A Book of Love

Acknowledgements

First and foremost, I would like to thank Etan Jonathan Ifeld for having confidence in me and my book. This book could never have materialized without him.

I'd like to thank my faithful translator, Baruch Gefen, whose work preserved the book's original musicality.

To Bob Saxton, who edited this book lovingly and wisely – a very big thank you.

I'd also like to personally thank Deborah Hercun, Jillian Levick, Jo Lal, and Gail Jones from the bottom of my heart, and to express my appreciation for everyone at Watkins who laboured over my book.

Last but never least – I'd like to thank my agent, Vicki Satlow, and my dear friend Ziv Lewis for their confidence in this work and the numerous hours they spent working on this project.

Thank you!

This edition published in the UK and USA 2016 by
Watkins, an imprint of Watkins Media Limited
19 Cecil Court, London WC2N 4EZ

enquiries@watkinspublishing.com

Design and typography copyright © Watkins Media Limited 2016
Text copyright © Haim Shapira 2016

1 3 5 7 9 10 8 6 4 2

Managing Editor: Deborah Hercun
Editor: Bob Saxton
Designer: Gail Jones

Printed and bound in Bookwell, Finland

A CIP record for this book is available from the British Library

ISBN: 978-1-78028-967-0

www.watkinspublishing.com

Contents

Overture

Over the centuries many people have meditated on the fundamental questions of human existence. This book is a voyage of sorts to the valley of great questions. Along with us I bring wise thinkers and sages of all faiths, nations and ages to help us understand their ideas.

On our road trip, we will meet Antoine de Saint-Exupéry and Jane Austen, Ludwig Wittgenstein and Lewis Carroll, Sigmund Freud and Lea Goldberg, Seneca and Vincent van Gogh, Katharine Hepburn and Simone Weil, John Keats and King Solomon, Rabindranath Tagore and Thich Nhat Hanh, Wisława Szymborska and Walt Whitman, Friedrich Nietzsche and Leo Tolstoy – to name but a few.

We'll have a quiz on the meaning of life, investigate why numbers are so important and check just how much land Tolstoy needed to be happy. Nietzsche will guide us through the Thousand Masks experiment. We'll question women on what makes them happy and find out why the answers surprise men so much. We'll discover the connection between 'lesson' and 'less', and what Mark Twain thought of anger. Epicurus will present his recipe for a happy life. The Fox will teach the Little Prince about love and friendship.

This little book is meant to change your perspective on almost everything in your life – and primarily the concept of happiness. But, as you may know, there are no free rides in this world. Readers who wish to make the best of this book will have to be active: they will need to extrapolate from parts of the text, correct whatever mistakes they find, and expand on any ideas they like.

As serious and life-changing as the voyage to the land of the Things That Matter may be, it's no less important to enjoy the ride. Having realized in my own life that serious is not the opposite of amusing, I've made a serious effort to present you with an amusing book that deeply and profoundly discusses all the Things That Matter.

1.

Happiness Matters

Aristotle believed that 'Happiness is the meaning and purpose of life; the whole aim.' In modern times, however, we have all kinds of different ideas about what happiness is. Some of us must go bungee jumping to trigger our rush of joy, while others will find their bliss staying at home. Some of us are happy in a concert hall listening to classical music; while the cacophony of children in a playground could be music to the ears of others. Some people find elation when they solve a complicated equation; for others a cancelled maths class is a happy childhood memory. Dostoevsky's novels introduce us to characters who experience great happiness just knowing that they exist, others who enjoy being miserable, and even several whose greatest joy is to make others sad.

We do differ from one another, often greatly. But is one way of living right and another wrong?

We all want to be happy, but is happiness truly possible?

The Intention that man should be 'happy' is not included in the plan of 'Creation'.

Sigmund Freud

We shouldn't confuse happiness with *moments* or *periods* of happiness. People can be happy for two hours, two days, and even a whole year … but that tends to be it: happiness never seems to sustain itself indefinitely. (By the way, Woody Allen disagrees with me. He believes that periods of happiness are much shorter, and that if anyone is happy for more than two days in a row, it's only because someone is hiding something from him or her.)

In this chapter, we'll see why the path to happiness is very narrow, with room for one person alone. We'll join Heinrich Heine as he plans his day of grand happiness. We'll familiarize ourselves with peak moments in the lives of men and women, and try to understand the reason for the huge differences between them.

Before we hit the road and start our journey to happiness, here's a little piece of advice:

Happiness is a butterfly which, when pursued, is always just beyond your grasp, but which, if you will sit down quietly, may alight upon you.

Nathaniel Hawthorne

On Statistics and Cookbooks

If university students were surveyed on the most boring subject they've ever had to study, statistics would probably win first place. A student once told me that he never understood the need for anaesthetists when there's such an abundance of books on statistics. Before going into the operating theatre, he said, patients could be asked to read two or three pages from a carefully selected textbook, and soon they'd be totally desensitized and ready for open-heart surgery.

When I suggested this to some of my physician friends, they were, at first, very enthusiastic about inducing general anaesthesia without any shots or invasive procedures. But when I showed them some of the textbooks in question, their excitement faded quickly. 'The patients,' they said, yawning, 'might never awake from surgery.'

To ease the suffering of my students who must take classes in statistics, and to show them that the subject can actually be amusing and even interesting, I often send them out to conduct surveys on diverse and even bizarre subjects. Once I suggested they find out what types of books are published most prolifically. After visiting a few bookstores, the young surveyors came up with the following result:

(Wait – can you guess the result before you go on? It shouldn't be hard.)

Hold your breath. Drumroll please. 'And the winner is:

'Cookbooks!'

Not very surprising, huh? Some books present recipes for extra-tasty and easy-to-make pies, others offer extra work and tasteless pies, while some explain the ties between American pie and mathematical Pi (π). Some chefs are naked, while others wear fancy suits. There are big chefs who give little tips, and little chefs who tip big.

(Here's my little tip for you: If you're going out with someone who has an impressive collection of cookbooks, don't forget to reserve a table in your favourite eatery.)

Despite this tantalizing hors d'oeuvres, however, in fact I'm not going to discuss cookbooks at all (and I certainly don't intend to write one, since all I know how to do is boil an egg). Actually, instead of the winner, I want to discuss the runner-up in that survey I've just mentioned: happiness guides.

How to Be Happy Forever in Just Three Minutes

There are countless books that carry the word 'Happiness' in their title and promise their readers lasting bliss: the resolution of all anxiety and self-doubt and the attainment of profound tranquillity. Some of these books even go as far as claiming that a few minutes of practice a day is all we need to attain this sublime goal.

A few years back, my wife read *Happiness the Feng Shui Way* and subsequently reached the conclusion that I created a flow of negative energy through our house – not to mention the fact that I did not match our furniture at all. I spent an entire week pointing out mistakes in the book to her and proving that I was no source of energy at all, let alone negative energy. In the end, we bought a new set of living room furniture.

What do you think about this kind of book? More often than not, when someone poses a 'What do you think …?' question, they follow it with a piece of their mind. So: let me tell you what I think about them.

Attempting to maintain objectivity, I decided not to read any self-help books of this kind. After all, once you read a book there's a chance you'll feel a personal connection with it, which might cloud your judgment. So rather than actually read them, I decided to leaf through a few instead.

I soon reached the following conclusion: in most cases, reading how-to-be-happy books will not make you happier (though it will help some of them become how-to-get-rich-fast books for their authors). Let me give you the main two of the many reasons that this is so:

There's Empirical Proof That How-to-Be-Happy Books Are Useless

If just a shred of the promises made in many of those books came true, the world would be knee-deep in incomprehensible quantities of bliss. We all know that this is not the case.

Knowing 'How to' Offers No Edge in the Search for Happiness

Knowledge is a must when you try to solve a differential equation, prepare truffle pie á la Robuchon or send a rocket into space. It's quite useless when you seek happiness. Let me explain. Leafing through one of those how-to guides, I came upon an amazingly wise piece of advice: 'Rise every morning with a big smile and in an excellent mood.' How lucky I was that the authors chose to share this insight with me. Before I stumbled upon this wonderful idea, I used to think that I should rise every morning with a sharp pain in my left kidney, feeling deeply depressed. Now I knew I'd been wrong all along.

The impact of such advice is equal to the impact of a 'Have a nice day!' bestowed upon you by a shopkeeper. Of course, this exhortation won't really make your day nice. Knowing the right thing to do is not really helpful. Smokers know they should quit, but how does that physiologically cure their nicotine addiction?

These books are so popular, of course, not so much because of the advice they contain but because many readers identify with the lifestyle described: 'Yes, of course, that is so true. I really should smile broadly every morning and do a good thing at least once a day.' Strangely, though, these how-to books in fact leave us wondering: Now, *how* do I do that? That's the big question.

In any event, I believe that there are no organized trips to happiness. Different people need different travel guides. I even doubt that the narrow path that leads to happiness offers enough room for one person. We are so different from each other that not even an organized trip to, say, Italy could satisfy every participant's desires. While some visitors to Rome would want to see the Sistine Chapel and feast on a variety of local pasta dishes and red wines, others would want to link up with their fellow countrymen for a chinwag about baseball and chomp on red meat in the local hamburger joints.

Although, as we can see, organized tours by their nature are sadly lacking in promise when it comes to individual fulfilment, perhaps there are some general navigation rules that could help us find the path to happiness if we could summon enough self-reliance to travel alone? In other words, are there learnable truths that are valid for most people when it comes to finding bliss?

Here is a nice exercise. Try asking yourself: Assuming that everything is possible, what would be the shape of the happiest day of your life?

This no simple question, so I should like you to take a few moments before you reply.

While you're thinking, let me tell you what the poet Heinrich Heine might have said about this very question.

The Happiest Day of My Life (a short essay that Heine never wrote)
The happiest day of my life would start when I slowly wake up in a wonderfully designed wooden cottage, up in the Swiss Alps. I would

leisurely get out of bed, stretch, scratch, yawn, and approach the breakfast table. Following my nose, I'd find a freshly baked baguette on which I generously spread sweet butter. Gently, I bite into the crispy bread and take a long sip from the freshly made Italian coffee that my servants have brought.

Then I walk up to the window and feast my eyes on the small, glimmering, turquoise lake in the valley below. My gaze travels down the mountain trail that leads to my cabin as I take in the snow-peaked mountains and their reflection in the lake.

Yes, this is bliss, but it is not yet perfect. What does a poet and a thinker like me need now? Well, if God wants to make me really happy, here is the little extra something I'd need to make this day absolutely exquisite: between the cottage and the lake I'd like to see a tree with my enemies dangling from the branches. Yes! The cottage, lake view, sweet butter spread over the fresh baguette, and my haters hanging in the treetops. Nothing could beat that!'

God will forgive me. That's His business.

Heinrich Heine

I quite sympathized with Heine, up to the point about the hanging tree. I don't want to see anyone hanging from anything, let alone trees. It doesn't make me happy, not in the slightest. During one of my lectures, however, a member of the audience loved the idea. In fact, he said, a small country such as Israel doesn't have enough trees to carry everyone he'd like to hang. Now, try telling this man that he should rise every morning with a smile.

As I pointed out before, people are quite different from one another, and have very different dreams and wishes. I once conducted a workshop on 'positive thinking'' for the employees of a large hi-tech firm, and discovered three interesting facts:

Fact 1

People don't really know what they want. It took some of the participants as long as 15 minutes just to start writing.

Fact 2

The best person to spend your happiest day with is not necessarily your partner.

Fact 3

We Don't Know What Will Make Us Happy.

Leafing through those guides to happiness, I stumbled on a truly excellent book by Daniel Gilbert: *Stumbling on Happiness* (Random House, 2006). It doesn't presume to guide us to happiness, but rather explains – based on a huge amount of up-to-date psychological studies – why we cannot know what will make us happy (not even if we crave a state-of-the-art 3D plasma TV, a fancy car or a new kitchen). If you don't know where you're going, Gilbert goes on to assert, how will you ever get there? What if you're headed the wrong way?

> You can't always get what you want.
>
> Sir Michael Philip (Mick) Jagger and Keith Richards (co-writers)

> That's not the problem, I think. The problem is, you can't always know what you want.
>
> Daniel Gilbert (as he might have said)

There are only two tragedies in life: one is not getting what
one wants, and the other is getting it.

Oscar Wilde

Well, it seems clear that you won't find the key to happiness in standard
self-help books and, unfortunately, not in this book either. As already
stated in the Overture, the little book you're holding now has a different
function. It's meant to change your perspective on almost everything in
your life – and primarily the concept of happiness.

We cannot teach people anything: we can only help them
discover it within themselves.

Galileo Galilei

Three Philosophical Principles

Vasily Rozanov, sometimes known as 'Rasputin of the Intellectuals', is
one of the most controversial writers and philosophers of pre-revolution
Mother Russia. Rozanov believed that life teaches us many things every
day, but regrettably we, the students, are inattentive and absent-minded.

In the following pages, I'd like to introduce you to three very basic and
really important philosophical principles, but before you start reading,
here's some travel advice.

As we've already seen, knowing what to do and actually doing it are
two very different things. Many who have found the path soon discovered
that, as hard as it was to find, it's even harder to follow.

A book is a mirror: if an ass peers into it, you can't expect
an apostle to look out.

Georg Christoph Lichtenberg

First Principle:

It's OK to Do Nothing While Munching on a Little Something

We're all familiar with this feeling: you wake up in the morning, and the first thought that comes to your mind is that the best thing to do now is to get right back between the sheets, for just two more hours … or five, or ten. The German philosopher Arthur Schopenhauer even believed this tendency to be proof that life is no picnic. If our lives were such a great celebration, we'd be jumping out of bed even before we completely opened our eyes.

I wake up every morning at nine and grab for the morning paper. Then I look at the obituary page. If my name is not on it, I get up.

Benjamin Franklin

A man may awake in the morning, but morning does not awake in him.

David Avidan

When I awake in the morning and feel no morning awake in me, I call my faculty secretary and tell her to cancel everything planned for the day because my back is killing me. (I have to lie a little, because every eyebrow would be raised in my academic circle if I called in to say that today I won't be showing up for work because no morning awoke in me.)

It is awfully hard work doing nothing.

Oscar Wilde

I totally agree with wise and witty Oscar. Doing nothing is both awfully hard and a truly wonderful adventure. Let me explain this better with a short story.

One day I was invited to give a lecture on game theory at a conference that was held in a seaside resort town. Since I was supposed to give my lecture on a Thursday, I felt I would need to recover from it over the weekend, and so I stayed in the hotel. On Friday morning, after a huge breakfast (that Pooh would have relished), I went down to the swimming pool to bask in the sun and do nothing. Amazingly enough, I failed miserably.

Here's what my brain said: 'Nu, Haim? What's with this sitting and doing nothing? Why don't you at least grab a book? Read an article on differential topology or the Mandelbrot fractal. Is this not a great time finally to start reading Joyce's *Ulysses* all the way through, or some other classic? Why don't you write another PhD thesis? Oh, I know – go listen to Mahler's Eighth or Ravel's G major piano concerto. Perhaps really you should take this opportunity to decide what you want to be when you grow up? Why are you wasting time lying here by the pool when your basement back home is such a mess? OK, you should at least exercise a little. Swim a little. Swimming is good for you. You really must lose those love handles ...'

And so my brain would not let me enjoy even a minute of idleness. After all, it isn't really hard to do nothing. Many of us can. The hard part is doing nothing without feeling guilty about it.

When I realized that my guilt pangs wouldn't leave me alone, I decided to work out, and engaged in agonizing exercises for quite a while. Let me tell you: I'm proud to say that today I can do nothing for a week and enjoy every moment of it! So perhaps our happiest moments are those mornings when we wake up but stay in bed a little longer, spoiling ourselves with doing nothing and daydreaming under a warm blanket? I recommend you try this the first chance you have.

Quite a few people, however, just don't get this idea and put forward the bizarre argument:

'Haim, doing nothing is silly. You're wasting time.'

Time, I always reply, is wasting anyway. No matter what I do or don't, time is wasting. That is the very nature of time.

Winnie-the-Pooh, for example, is never in a hurry and simply does what he wants to do. Paradoxically, although Pooh never exerts himself particularly hard, he does manage to make his wishes come true, and he has many adventures: he finds the North Pole, helps Eeyore find his tail, makes up poems, and flies with the help of a balloon.

The Chinese call this principle *Wu Wei*. Wu means 'without' and Wei means 'effort' – the main idea of this Taoist principle is that we need to know when to act and when to let things just happen. And even when we act, we should go about this effortlessly, the way trees grow or waves roll. The best rendition of this principle I've found in English is 'creative quietude'.

In our day and age, most of us spend most of our time 'doing' and devote little time to just 'being'. Pooh exemplifies the essential quality of 'being', and clearly enjoys himself greatly.

Of course, I'm not advocating absolute inaction. I'm speaking about the fundamental balancing act: while we work and create, which is our very essence and the purpose of our existence in this world, we must find time to enjoy our mere presence, our 'being' here, and relish it.

And now to something not entirely different: four new versions of the Tale of the Ant and the Grasshopper. If you're too curious and already dying to know what my second principle is, you are welcome to skip the following passages and come back to visit Ant and Grasshopper when you feel like it.

The Ant and the Grasshopper, Version 1
(a fable by Aesop, with four different morals)

The Grasshopper spent all summer and autumn singing, dancing and drinking with friends, while the Ant worked hard and stored up food for the winter.

When winter came, the starving Grasshopper went to the Ant and asked for something to eat. The Ant not only gave him nothing, but even reprimanded him for his laziness.

Here is the moral of the story, according to several wise men:

Aesop: *Go to the ant, you sluggard, consider her ways, and learn wisdom.*

La Fontaine: *Good planning is half the job.*

Krilov, the Russian storyteller: *Think before you act.*

Dani Kerman, the Israeli cartoonist: *If you enjoy singing and dancing, you should pick better friends than such uncivilized ants.*

The Ant and the Grasshopper, Version 2

(an alternative account inspired by Positive Psychology)

The Grasshopper spent all summer and autumn singing, dancing and drinking with friends, while the Ant worked hard and stored up food for the winter.

When winter came, the Ant sat in her food-packed house and was getting really bored. One day she heard a car pulling into her driveway. The eager Ant opened the door and was amazed to see the Grasshopper stepping out of a bright-red Ferrari, wearing a designer suit and smoking a Cuban cigar.

'Where did you get all that?' the hard-working but simple Ant asked.

'Well, Ma'am, I sang and danced and played my fiddle until my agent got me a winter job with the Paris Opera for a large fistful of dollars. I'm going there now. Want to come?'

'Sure,' said the Ant. 'I'll go to the Paris Opera with you, and I'll look up that La Fontaine dude, then I'll give him a piece of my mind: hard work only pays in fables he copied from Aesop.'

'Done deal. We'll meet him at Angelina's. They serve an amazing chestnut tart.' Saying this, Grasshopper opened the door of his Ferrari door for her.

The Ant and the Grasshopper, Version 3
(the Walt Disney version)

The Grasshopper spent all summer and autumn singing, dancing and drinking with friends, while the Ant worked hard and stored up food for the winter.

When winter came, Grasshopper went to Ant to ask for some food. Ant said, 'I have to consult the Ant Queen. Come back tomorrow.'

On the next day, when Grasshopper showed up, Ant told him it had been decided he would be given some food, provided he moved into the ants' winter quarters. At 7.30 every night he would have to sing and dance and play his fiddle for them all. Too hungry even to consider whether he had an alternative, Grasshopper accepted the Queen's terms.

Soon the ants became very fond of Grasshopper. Every night his shows would turn into a huge ball, with the ants feasting and dancing to his tunes. And every night, when the concert ended, Grasshopper would retire to his chambers with two beautiful ants, one on each arm.

The Ant and the Grasshopper, Version 4
(Eeyore's version)

The Grasshopper spent all summer and autumn singing, dancing and drinking with friends, while the Ant worked hard and stored up food for the winter.

When winter came, the Grasshopper went to the Ant and begged for some food. The Ant reprimanded him for his lazy ways, but before she could say everything she had to say, a man who was walking through the forest accidentally stepped on both the Ant and the Grasshopper, squashing them. C'est la vie.

At this point, I'll leave the ant and grasshopper to rest in peace and move on to discuss the second principle of Pooh's life philosophy.

Second Principle:
Anger Is Punishing Yourself for the Stupidity of Others; or Anger is Punishing Yourself for Your Own Stupidity

> It takes me a long time to lose my temper, but once lost,
> I could not find it with a dog.
>
> Mark Twain

Very few people know this, but one of the world's greatest experts on anger management is Baruch Spinoza, the great Jewish philosopher. The following sentence is a summary of Spinoza's philosophy of anger:

> Never get angry, or never forgive.

Let me explain. According to the great Jewish philosopher, before you get angry with someone, you should consider whether you intend to forgive this person sometime in the future. That person may be a fine candidate for your anger right now, but if you feel you could ever forgive them – in a week, a month, six months, or a year – it's best to forgive them right now and avoid the unnecessary rage and agony.

> Anger is an acid that can do more harm to the vessel in
> which it is stored than to anything on which it is poured.
>
> Mark Twain

Spinoza, therefore, treated time in a very special way in his version of philosophy – in fact, he tried to see everything from the point of view of eternity. One of his conclusions was that if you're ever going to forgive anyone, your anger today is illogical. It's totally unnecessary and even absurd.

This view received unexpected support:

One should not lose one's temper unless one is certain of getting more and more angry to the end.

William Butler Yeats

Spinoza, however, was not naïve. He knew that certain things can never be forgiven, and so he stated that if you do decide to be angry and bear a grudge for the rest of your life, then fine, go right ahead. You must be careful, though, because there's a little-big catch here. If you happened to become angry with someone and then chose to forgive them after 30 minutes (if you were just a little angry) or 30 years (if you were terribly angry), you would have made a mistake and should not have been angry to begin with.

It is critical for us to adopt Spinoza's attitude in our closest relationships. After all, what are the chances that a parent would be mad at his offspring for the rest of his life? Can siblings be angry with each other forever? What is the point of being angry with someone for a day, a week or even a year if you will eventually forgive them?

As always, all this is easier said than done.

One of the reasons why Spinoza was so greatly appreciated – even by his philosopher colleagues, who called him a 'philosopher's philosopher' – was the fact that he walked his talk and lived according to his teachings.

Good for him, but we are not Spinoza. It's much harder for us.

***

The Dalai Lama teaches a method that should help us not to lose our temper. He says that we must distinguish between people and their deeds. We have no reason to be angry with people, because no one's life on Earth is easy. We may, however, be *upset* about people's actions. I tried the Dalai Lama method, but my achievements were unimpressive. When someone makes me mad (which happens rarely, but does happen), I find it impossible to forget that person and focus my anger on his or her actions alone. I find the two inseparably intertwined.

Happiness and Other Small Things of Absolute Importance

So here's a human piece of advice:

If you are angry … count to ten.
If you are really angry … swear.

Mark Twain

The Straight Story

Directed by David Lynch, *The Straight Story* is a film that tells the story of Alvin Straight (consider the numerous meanings of this name), an elderly World War II veteran who lives with his daughter Rose, a kind-hearted woman with a mental disability. He has an estranged brother, Lyle, whom he has not seen for many years because they have had a falling out of sorts.

One day Alvin learns that his brother has suffered a stroke and decides to visit him before it's too late for both of them. Alvin's legs and eyes are too weak for him to receive a driving licence for any conventional vehicle, so he decides to make the trip on his John Deere lawn tractor. The 240-mile voyage from Laurens, Iowa, to Mount Zion, Wisconsin, takes him six weeks.

When the brothers finally meet, you can see that they've missed each other (actually, you can see that in the eyes of Richard Farnsworth and Harry Dean Stanton, the wonderful actors). The two deeply regret their years of alienation and anger (and, absurdly enough, they can't even remember what drove them apart in the first place).

Nothing is straight in this story.

In every minute of anger, you lose 60 seconds of peace.

Ralph Waldo Emerson

Admittedly, I still have a lot to learn about anger management (and I'm trying), but as is often the case I learned quite a lot from the following incident, in which I tried to teach someone else about the harm of getting angry.

Taxi Driver 1 (not Martin Scorsese's)

One day I hailed a taxi (with its driver). As we were coasting down the highway, another car cut us up wildly, seriously risking the lives of the taxi's occupants – not to mention, the maverick driver himself and his car. The taxi driver became really angry and started cursing and screaming. After a while, as I realized that he wasn't about to stop, I tried to explain that what he was doing was completely illogical. I said that the crazy driver was probably already home, sitting in his warm bathtub, playing with his rubber duckie. I went on to say that the only people who were really being punished at this time were the two of us: me, because I had to listen to his loud rant, and him, because the tantrum might cause him real physical harm. He was convinced. 'I will never lose my temper again,' he declared. 'I will never give them the satisfaction! They will see me get mad over my dead body!' His voice nearly shattered the windows.

Anger is punishing yourself for the stupidity of others.

Common knowledge

(Of course, common knowledge and common sense are so not commonly found.)

A physician once told me that recent scientific studies clearly show that people who are easily irritated and lose their temper simply live shorter lives. How surprising is that?

I make a habit of getting angry only when there's a chance that my rage will change something.

So, let us pray:

God grant me the serenity to accept the things I cannot change; courage to change the things I can; and wisdom to know the difference.

Reinhold Niebuhr, 'The Serenity Prayer' (1943)

Taxi Driver 2 (again, unrelated to Scorsese's work)

One day I was in a Tel Aviv taxi again (I used to be a serial passenger), and this time we hit heavy traffic. As we were crawling to our destination, the driver noticed a car that passed us (and everyone else) from the right, driving on the hard shoulder. The furious taxi driver unleashed a few sentences that this book can do without. After he calmed down a little, he said: 'What disgusting people Israelis are, every last one of them. They violate the law as if they were in a rush to save their grandma whose house was on fire. Tell me,' he turned to me, 'why are all Israelis so rude?' (He used another word too.)

It was a great opportunity for me to give the man a lesson in statistical deduction.

'Is it possible that your conclusion is a little off the mark?' I asked.

'What do you mean? Why am I wrong?' he countered.

'Well, are you driving on the hard shoulder?' I started, presenting my case.

'No, I'm not.'

'And is the car in front of us doing anything illegal?' I went on.

'No,' he said, sounding very suspicious.

'I hope you noticed that the car on our left is doing fine too. The truth is that only one car violated the law. We saw no one else driving on the hard shoulder, did we?' I started closing my argument.

'What are you trying to say?' he asked, less angry now.

'What funny people we are,' I said. 'We easily notice anything bad or irritating, but ignore the good things. Dozens of drivers around us did not cross that yellow line, but you never said that it's nice to have so many patient and polite motorists around us. You saw only one (one!) driver who violated the law, and immediately concluded that not only are all Israeli motorists evil, but that all Israelis are wrongdoers. Isn't it amazing?' I rested my solid case.

Thus end my taxi tales.

Now try this.

Please check how many TV shows you can think of that present us with good people. And why is it that every newscast carries so many reports about negative things that take place, while a little show about people who do good, which was aired on one of the commercial channels, was soon axed on account of low ratings? (I believe that the viewers switched to other channels in search of 'nicer' things to watch, such as stories of a wife-killing husband, a young man who beat an old one, and an abusive mother.) What does that say about us?

In some of his finest short stories the great Russian writer Leo Tolstoy implicitly posed the following question:

Why do people so easily, without a second thought, believe everything bad they hear about others, but cannot believe the good things they hear?

If you were honest, you'd admit that good old Count Leo was right. This is indeed a regular thinking pattern of ours.

If you still doubt it, here's proof. Suppose a newspaper or Internet site should report tomorrow that Haim Shapira, author of the book in your hands, was arrested on suspicion of spying for Russia. I know exactly what the reactions would be.

People would say things like:

'I knew there was something suspicious about him the minute I saw him.'

'It does not surprise me at all.'

'He has a Russian accent and he keeps quoting Russian writers. How come he knows Tolstoy, Nabokov and Visotzky so well?'

'He's also good at maths and plays piano, which is typically Russian. Besides, all Russians are spies.'

Here's a partial answer to Tolstoy's question:

> If we had no faults of our own, we would not take so much
> pleasure in noticing those of others.
>
> François de La Rochefoucauld

I want to translate this wise saying by the French aristocrat from English to simple English:

> The more flaws one sees in others, the more flaws
> one possesses.

Proper Disclosure

Many believe that a man is as big as the things that make him angry. A nice saying, I say, but not entirely right. I believe that Heraclitus was right when he said that character is fate. A wise person should not get angry, but that's just a theory. I've heard that Spinoza and a few other wise men did manage to avoid anger by drawing upon their wisdom, but they are a negligible minority. We ordinary mortals cannot do that. As Emerson said, people boil at different temperatures that were determined without consulting them.

Before we move on to the third principle, I'd like to give you an insight that is based on decades of observing others and, mainly, myself. Soon after I turned 40, I fully realized that we should not delude ourselves into believing that we can easily discard unwanted emotions. Believing we can is hubris par excellence – not everything follows man's will and desire.

Once, surfing the Internet, I came across an ad whose banner read: 'Anger Management – Getting Rid of Anger Is Easy'. Though this was nicely phrased, I did not buy the product. Learning to manage one's emotions is a lifelong endeavour. Only very young people, or older ones who didn't grow wiser with time, can believe that they can fill their hearts with anger and animosity at will, or may make peace with everything should they so desire.

Wise people know that in the battle between emotions and thoughts, the former will almost always prevail. Either way, being one of the greatest obstacles on people's paths to better and proper lives, anger is too important to be set aside. And so let us decide that we will analyse our spells of rage later (when we're more tranquil).

Third Principle:
Unstoppable Minds Can Be Stopped

My grandmother died peacefully aged 101. She was blessed with some charming qualities. She had many friends, was very generous, never green-eyed and knew how to cheer others up and help them get rid of unfounded worries and false anxieties.

She had a bright sense of humour. I must tell you one of her quips. One day, my mother caught grandma, who was almost 100 at the time, talking to herself. At first, granny was embarrassed, but when she recovered, she said: "Yes, I talk to myself. That's true. It's not because I'm crazy, but because no one in your house is as wise as me. There's no one else to talk to here."

Perhaps therein lies the secret of her longevity. Either way, her philosophy of life closely resembles that of a Greek philosopher who lived fewer years than she, but many years before her.

On Epicureanism: 'Let Us Assume that the Earth Will Quake'

The main portion of the philosophy of Epicurus (who lived in the third century BC) deals with the teachings of contentment. Epicurus wrote quite extensively (more than 300 scrolls, according to Diogenes Laertius), but very few of his writings survived. The most complete work we have is *Principal Doctrines* – a collection of some 40 aphorisms on ethics. Only segments remain of his other works, but they all reflect unique philosophical courage, humanity and nobility (Epicurus apparently walked his talk).

The proponents of Judaism and Christianity did not appreciate his works. Christians fought against him because he did not believe in divine intervention or the idea that the human soul is eternal (Dante placed Epicurus and his disciples in his *Inferno*, canto 10, circle 6), while Jews use the name Epicurus as an adjective, referring to persons who defy faith and God, or sometimes just to free spirits in general.

Tetrapharmakos

These are Epicurus' four principles – his *Tetrapharmakos* – for healing the mind:

1. We need not fear God.
2. We need not fear death.
3. Evil can be tolerated.
4. Good can be acquired.

Below, I shall briefly discuss the first three and then elaborate on the fourth.

We Need Not Fear God

There is no reason to fear God because, even though God exists, Epicurus maintains that there is no divine intervention. Humans are not important enough for God to bother punishing or rewarding us. After all, is thinking that God is involved in our personal affairs not committing the sin of vanity at the highest level?

When we talk to God, we're praying.
When God talks to us, we're schizophrenic.

Jane Wagner (Lily Tomlin's comedy writer and life partner)

God exists, but I am an atheist.

Unknown comedian

I should like mercy, not justice, to guide God.

Miguel de Cervantes

I tremble for my country when I reflect that God is just; that
his justice cannot sleep forever.

Thomas Jefferson

Whether or not God is dead, it is impossible to keep silent
about him who was there for so long.

Elias Canetti

2.

We Need Not Fear Death

For most humans, our greatest fear is probably death. Epicurus cannot
understand this.

While we are here, death is not; once death arrives,
we are no longer here. We never meet death, so what's
to fear?

Inspired by Epicurus

3.

Evil Can Be Tolerated

Speaking with great mercy and compassion, Epicurus urges miserable
people who suffer from deformities, diseases, old age and agonizing
fatal illnesses to summon their courage when dealing with pain and the
circumstances they cannot escape. As I noted above, Epicurus was true to
his own word. He was very ill most of his life, but he wouldn't let his pain
break his spirit.

The feeling of pain does not linger continuously in the flesh;

rather, the sharpest pain is present for the shortest time.

Epicurus

Epicurus even agreed with the following saying of the great philosopher of the night:

That which does not kill us, makes us stronger.

Friedrich Nietzsche

Epicurus didn't say that life without sorrow is possible, but he aspired to deserve everything that happened to him in life.

My wounds existed before me, I was born to embody them.

Joe Bousquet

One last thing I'd like to mention about this third principle is that Epicurus did not really fear bodily pain, arguing that mental pain is greater. Physical pain exists only in the present, he claimed, while mental pain is mostly associated with the present but also with the past, and even the future.

Good Can Be Acquired

This principle is where Epicurus presents his recipe for happiness. As my intelligent readers may have already gathered, I'm not a great believer in 'happiness recipes'; but if we must have one, Epicurus' is my favourite.

First, Epicurus recommends friendship. He maintained that one cannot be wise without understanding that friendship is the greatest of values (I will discuss this later in the book).

Next, Epicurus speaks of two types of pain that hinder our happiness: physical and mental. Physical pain is expressed through bodily damage, hunger, thirst and cold, while mental pain comprises anxieties and fears. Tranquillity will come to us when we no longer feel pain, and that (according to him, of course) will put us on the road to happiness. Epicurus urges tranquillity of body and mind. He doesn't renounce pleasures, but suggests that we engage in them cautiously, because the pain that might follow them could be greater than the joy they bring.

Epicurus further warns us against the kinds of damage inflicted by greed, pursuit of honour and glory, lust, gluttony, envy, presumptuousness, and hubris or vanity.

As noted above, Epicurus was not naïve, which is why he also pointed out that people cannot acquire many possessions through honesty (what else is new?), and that acquisitiveness is not worth the effort because all possessions bring is mental unrest.

Nothing is enough for the man to whom enough is too little.

Epicurus

Who is rich? He who rejoices in his portion.

Ethics of the Fathers

The things you own end up owning you. It's only after you lose everything that you're free to do anything.

Tyler Durden's insight from the movie *Fight Club*

As far as mental pain (that is, anxiety) is concerned, Epicurus believed that we mostly worry for no reason at all. I believe he would gladly endorse this:

No enemy can even come close to man's worst enemy: his thoughts. Something my grandmother taught me.

I believe that both Epicurus and my grandma are correct. Just consider the strange things that trouble our minds. What is the universe made of? Is it finite or infinite? Is it expanding or shrinking? Are there parallel universes? Is there intelligent life on Mars? (Of course, many people have more earthly concerns, such as paying the bills, the state of the economy, their struggling children, sickness within the family, and the like.)

In fact, all that Epicurus wants is to live in tranquillity and try to be happy; and if that's not possible, at the very least he wants to suffer as little as possible.

Wouldn't you like to suffer as little as possible? According to this wise Greek sage, one of the most important things we can do in life is to assume that 'that tree will not fall on us'. After all, we worry the most about things that never happen.

Let me explain with an example.

Imagine you're on a plane, flying to a vacation on an island in Thailand. How enjoyable it is to spend your time in the air engaged in pleasant thoughts such as: what if the plane crashes? and if we don't crash, what if a tsunami turns our hotel into a floating guest house? Oh, I just know I'll eat something bad and get sick, or have a heart attack, or go numb from a massage. I'm sure my boss will seize the opportunity to fire me while I'm on leave. What if my daughter runs off with an Eskimo modelling agent? And what if the food they serve on the plane doesn't agree with me and I have to run to the bathroom throughout my whole vacation?

I can only hope that none of you entertains thoughts that even slightly resemble these. Epicurus argues that there's no logical or probabilistic reason to think this way, simply because almost none of those troubling things will actually happen.

Let's think this through:

First, I'm sure we can agree that if, while airborne, the pilot were suddenly to announce that we were about to crash-land in the ocean, it would be stupid to worry about a tsunami. Let it come, for all we care.

See? We worried for nothing.

Second, if a tsunami should hit our resort, who cares if our boss decides to fire us? Let him have a ball. We couldn't care less.

Third, there's absolutely no way that the following scenario could possibly happen. Flying over the ocean, the pilot announces we're crashing (that is, heading for a drowning), and that we're about to fall right into a colossal tsunami. Terror makes our heart beat erratically, and now we're having a massive coronary. As we reach our hand to our chest, we feel a lump and just know this is a malignant tumour. We tremble with horror – but wait! It's our mobile vibrating. The boss is calling to let us know we're fired. Then there's a call waiting, and it's our daughter letting us know she'll be spending the rest of her life in an igloo. Now we feel nauseous – dreadful airline food is upsetting our stomach.

Not even Eeyore the gloomy donkey could believe in such a scenario.

There is zero probability those things could happen all together, and so … there's no reason to worry about them.

Epicurus says that whatever is meant to happen will happen, one way or another. This too, he feels, is no reason to worry, because the trouble that will hit us will be mostly of the unexpected kind – namely, things we never even considered. For example, I don't know where you are right now, but if you're sitting under a huge chandelier, I would suggest you find a better spot. Who knows what might happen?

(I hope you didn't panic and are now reading under a blanket holding a flashlight.)

The main problem with Epicurus' theory is that it's very hard to tell ourselves not to worry without a reason, and it's even harder to put the idea into practice. We often give ourselves excellent advice, but we very rarely listen.

Man's greatest tragedy is the fact that he has no brake that

could stop, when necessary, a thought or even the entire
thinking process.

Paul Valéry

Valéry is absolutely right. Our thinking minds really do run like cars
without brakes. We cannot stop our thoughts at will, not even for a moment.
We cannot stop thinking, but maybe we can have better thoughts? Keep
on reading.

Some Thoughts about Happiness, Pessimism and Childhood

As we know all too well, people in this world don't really 'live happily ever
after'. As we've seen, our old friend Sigmund Freud took the view that
happiness was not part of the world creation plan. And if there's a person
somewhere who is happy each and every moment of his life, I could refer
them to places where the best doctors treat this strange mental condition.

A *lifetime* of happiness! No man alive could bear it: it
would be hell on earth.

George Bernard Shaw, Man and Superman

No one can be happy 24/7/365 – that much is clear. We should understand,
however, that each of us is entitled to minutes of happiness, short moments
of grace, and glimpses of tranquillity. Sometimes we may even feel at
peace and satisfied with our life's course.

The simplistic idea, therefore, would be to recommend that everyone
make every possible and impossible effort to collect as many such
moments throughout their lives, because these are the things that matter.
The problem is that we cannot order such moments online and have them
custom-made. In fact, it's even possible that the very pursuit of happiness
might be the greatest obstacle on the road to happiness itself.

> If one were to build the house of happiness, the largest
> space would be the waiting room.

Jules Renard

To sum up, I'd say that there's an abyss between happiness and misery, and we all live in it most of the time.

Thinking about how rare the happy moments of our lives are, I was sad to realize that so many people don't even notice them when they actually happen. It's often the case that we realize we had a happy moment only after it's over, and time has provided us with a fresh perspective.

The great Russian writer Fyodor Dostoevsky wrote that what gets us through the most difficult moments is neither our upbringing nor the things we learned later in life. Our childhood memories keep us strong and help us go on. A particularly good childhood memory is the best medication against all the nasty things that await each and every one of us on the path of life.

My finest childhood memory includes my father. Where I grew up, come winter, the neighbourhood children used to speed down a snowy hill using all sorts of skis, sledges and even plastic bags. Most of the time, that hill was covered with a slippery mixture of snow and ice.

At the age of seven or eight, I was a chubby boy. My father had just bought me a wooden sledge and took me to that hill to try it.

When we reached the top, my dad positioned me on the sledge, gave me a few quick instructions, and cautioned me at length about the perils of sledging. When he was satisfied that I'd understood everything, he let go of my arm and I started happily sliding down the hill. But then I realized that my dad was running alongside me, trying to make sure nothing happened to me, and yelling instructions and words of caution. Now, I reached the bottom safe and sound. But my father slipped and fell a couple of times along the way. I mean, how could anyone even think of running down such a slippery, icy hill?

Everyone around us laughed at the spectacle, but I was deeply shamed. What could be more embarrassing for a child than having your father making a fool of himself and overprotecting you? I just wanted to disappear. Of course, I wanted to slide down that hill all over again as soon as I reached the bottom, but having my dad running awkwardly next to me did not seem like fun. I tried once again, created a similar scene, and gave it up for a while.

I would never have expected this back then, but every time I remember that day, my heart is filled with great joy, because the memory assures me that my dad cared about me and loved me dearly.

And now we make a giant leap, from my childhood memories to an intriguing logical inconsistency of some of the pessimistic philosophers: while many of them maintain that life is full of vanities and generally intolerable, they complain about it being too short and ending too fast. Isn't that weird? Incidentally, many of the pessimistic philosophers believe that pessimism is a mark of a superior intellect. It makes me wonder.

Years ago, I studied evolution and discovered that pessimism may be the result of evolution (amygdala is to blame). In the early days of humanity, when survival was paramount, we chose to believe that a rattling bush meant an approaching tiger, not that another tooth fairy got lost. So perhaps the pessimistic approach to life is our not-very-interesting thought default?

For the sake of full disclosure, I should say that I used to be an ardent believer in all kinds of pessimistic philosophers – from the Buddha to Arthur Schopenhauer. One I valued was Oswald Spengler, who simply said: 'Optimism is cowardice.' I admired the pessimistic and cynical witticisms of Gorgias, Franz Kafka, Sigmund Freud, Mark Twain, Anton Chekhov, and many others. With time I grew wiser, I believe, and today I hold that:

Pessimism is usually an expression of intellectual laziness.

Inspired by Colin Wilson

Consider for a moment how simple and yet true this short phrase is. Bear in mind how easy it is to be pessimistic and disappointed and angry all the time; to say that everyone is corrupt and things will always be bad; to declare that the world was corrupted and evil and silly when we were born, and that it will be just the same when we depart. Isaac Bashevis Singer once said that any idiot who spreads doomsday forecasts around may be glorified as a prophet. I, too, believe that one doesn't need an IQ of more than 17 to let the world know that things are bad and will get worse, and that the light at the end of the tunnel is an oncoming train, and that there's nowhere to run.

Anyone who has lived on this planet long enough knows that pessimism is the natural way to think. It requires no effort, like a rock rolling downhill. It's much harder to push the rock up the hill, to think positively. Just see the effort it takes to think like Pooh, to find a bit of magic and grace in everything. That is a mission worthy of the wise.

I believe that although in the long run the pessimist is always right, the optimist enjoys the ride.

You are where your thoughts are.
Make sure your thoughts are where you want to be.

The above aphorism may sound like it was taken from The Secret, but is attributed to Rabbi Nahman of Breslev, and mildly different versions of it were offered by the Buddha, Marcus Aurelius, Epictetus and Leo Tolstoy. I guess it was no great secret after all.

'We are where our thoughts are' is so true that it's no surprise that so many wise men reached the same insight independently of each other. The five I mentioned must be a drop in the ocean.

(The following paragraphs are an addendum, written especially for philosophy buffs or admirers of the Marquis de Sade. You can skip them if you wish, and resume your reading overleaf.)

The Marquis de Sade and the Stoics

The Stoic philosophers distinguished between 'situations' and 'events'. Situations are not up to us. They just happen and there is nothing we can do about them. A tsunami may wash you away; a meteorite could hit you while you're reading a book; a person who commits suicide jumping from a tall building might fall right on your head on the day you put on your best suit. You get the drift (optimistic situations can also happen, but we're less interested in them at the moment).

While a situation happens independently of us and we cannot control it, an 'event' is created by what we think about what is happening to us and how we react to various situations. In other words, we turn situations into events. According to the Stoics, a person is the sum total of his chosen reactions to situations that come his way – on the mental and on the practical level. Hence the Stoics' most important moral slogan: *Be worthy of anything that happens to you.*

Two novels by Sade, *Justine* and *Juliette*, which tell the stories of two sisters – one who is good and one who is not so good – brilliantly demonstrate the difference between a situation and an event. These two novels are not recommended reading for people who prize their sanity. I read them when my mind was boring me, so I decided to get out of it for a while. When I returned, I brought back many interesting ideas, but ever since then I've spent my time in my newly expanded mind and never ventured out.

An initial, superficial reading creates the impression that Justine is the good sister and so, following Sade's twisted logic, every possible and impossible disaster shall befall her. With the Marquis, no good deed goes unpunished. At the same time, the evil sister Juliette does extremely well and is highly successful. Nevertheless, a second reading of the two novels (which is even less recommended than the first) reveals a very surprising fact. The two sisters encounter almost the same set of situations, and while good sister Justine suffers greatly from the situations that Sade drops on her head, bad sister Juliette chooses to enjoy very similar situations, and does so, big time.

Back to our business. Some people think that the fact that they complain all the time about everything they see or hear makes them appear extremely wise. However:

> It's bad taste to be wise all the time, like being at a perpetual funeral.
>
> D H Lawrence, 'Peace and War' (a poem)

Last Tango in Venice

A few years back, my wife and I went on a trip to Italy with a couple of our friends. I love touring Italy and do it as often as I can. It has a good influence on my psyche. Early on in our trip, while on our way from Rome to the Dolomites, we had a chance to spend two days in Venice. On our second day there, I realized that our tour companion was a very 'wise' man. While we were cruising the Venice waterways, our friend decided to share his great wisdom with us. First, he let us know that the city was crumbling and will disappear under water in 30 to 40 years, tops. After he'd finished smashing Venice to smithereens, he called our attention to the fact that the sewage system of the city of palaces was badly built (I can only hope that none of my readers ever trouble their minds too much with Venice's sewage planning and construction). After he'd crumbled Venice and flooded it with waste water, he pointed out that the Montepulciano wine we were served at dinner the night before was not a 1997, as we requested, but a 2001, or even – Lord have mercy! – a 2003. We were cheated, he said.

And so this friend of ours kept pumping facts into my head as if he were determined slowly but surely to ruin my Italian vacation. Alas, the man who knew it all did not know one thing: that I knew almost everything he knew. The difference between us was that I – following in the footsteps of my great teacher Winnie-the-Pooh – chose to look at everything through softer, lighter, rosier glasses. I know that Venice is slowly crumbling, but that's part of its magic. (After all, they have built Venice replicas in Vegas and Macau, and they *do not* crumble, but do they have the magic? Of course not.)

Even if the sewage system was built badly, it's been working for hundreds of years. I mean, give them a break! When was the last time you bought a product with even a 100-year warranty?

Yes, they cheated us with the wine (I also noticed), but so what? At least our waiter gave us some thought, which is nice too. Although I would have loved him to think of us beyond 'How do I trick these suckers?' and it's a shame that he chose that thought to include us in, I refuse to let such small things ruin the few beautiful moments that, as we've seen, are so hard to come by and collect. After all, these are the moments that will stay in our memory's scrapbook. As a wise man once said: 'Good memories create the Heaven from which no one can deport us.'

Ever since that trip, our friend has called me occasionally, trying to find out where and when I'll be traveling next, and every time he hears the same answer: 'Sorry, I just got back.' That was our last tango.

Time for a break.

Tea and biscuits and honey would be welcome.

Surveys, Lies and Moments of Happiness

Reporter: 'Are you happy, Sir?'
Charles De Gaulle: 'What do you take me for, an idiot?'

The Big (False) Happiness Survey

One of the most fascinating, and even perhaps one of the most important surveys I ever conducted, was questioning people about their happiest moments. The people being surveyed were given a blank sheet of paper and asked to describe their happiest moment ever. I gave them five minutes to do that, which is plenty, and told them that if more than one such moment knocked at their memory door, they should write them all down and rate the moments by their intensity.

Before I share my findings with you, I'd like to ask you, dear reader, to take five minutes and consider: What was your happiest moment? Which moment came in second? Do you have a third? How many could you jot down in five minutes?

I'd like to add that happy moments change shade over time. We've all had moments of joy that later turned out to be less than happy, but we've also had moments we realized were happy only years later.

> One must be a God to tell successes from failures without making a mistake.
>
> Anton Chekhov

Take your time and write.

Joy? What Joy?
It saddened me to discover that quite a few grown-ups turned in a blank sheet – that is, they couldn't think of a single happy moment in their lives, or they chose not to respond to the question, which is also sad. Some of my students were unable to remember one moment of joy in their past, but thankfully they are young and there's still hope for them.

> Happiness clearly doesn't exist; still, one day you wake up and find it's gone.
>
> Anonymous

> We are never as happy or as unhappy as we imagine.
>
> François de La Rochefoucauld

I wondered about the people who couldn't find a single moment of happiness. What had they been doing with their lives? Today, I know I was wrong to wonder. As noted earlier, our ability to experience moments of joy (and many other things) is to a large extent genetic (it's our parent's fault again). Eeyore knows that.

Men and Women

I further discovered from the surveys that men and women often experience such different moments of joy that I began to wonder if they even live on the same planet and breathe the same air. This reminded me of a friend who is a gender studies professor and a fighting feminist. Her car is decorated with a bumper sticker that reads: 'I think, therefore I am single.' (Did you ever consider that, Descartes?)

> If you want to sacrifice the admiration of a million men for the criticism of one, go ahead, get married.
>
> Katharine Hepburn

In any event, this friend of mine totally disagreed and was even a little angry with me when I told her about the huge differences I found between men and women. She argued that there are no substantial differences at all, except perhaps for the fact that men like women while women like men (at least for the most part).

I insisted that there are actually thousands of large and small differences between the genders. One of those differences is based on this simple fact: women want many things from one man; men want one thing from many women.

This is where things start getting complicated, which is why I always ask the people I survey to note their gender.

Let us begin reviewing the findings of my survey. Being a gentleman, I'll chivalrously declare: ladies first.

What Makes Women Happy?

I've pondered what women want all my life. Yet, even now

that I'm old and wise, I don't have the slightest idea.

Inspired by Sigmund Freud

I reviewed responses supplied by female students who took various courses I gave – from Psychology and Genetics to Game Theory – and came upon no particularly fascinating findings. Here's a rather accidental collection of answers to the question, What has made you happiest? (I've picked randomly from my notes and typed these snippets in):

Skydiving with a cute instructor

Qualifying for studies here (*I can only hope said studies justified that*)

My cat recovered

I got to know myself

Watching the sunset on Ko Phi Phi

Taking a trip to South America (*Don't people just love to travel?*)

I met my boyfriend

I realized that my mythological ex still loved me! (*Exclamation mark in the original*)

A Vipassana retreat I attended

A trip I took to Costa Rica (*People really seem to like to travel*)

My first kiss (*Finally that!*)

A trip to New Zealand (*OK, I got it, people love to travel*)

Graduating in officers' school

Ménage à trois

The day I was proposed to

My trip to India (*Enough already*)

OK, this is getting old fast. I'm sure you get the drift.

Things became a little more interesting when I surveyed women who were a bit older. No breathtaking moments there either, mind you, but the interesting thing about slightly older women was the fact that there was almost no distribution of data at all. The majority of women spoke of the same experience as their happiest moment. Can you guess what it was?

I bet the girls did. I'm pretty sure the guys didn't.

The vast majority of women chose the moment they brought life into this world – the moment of giving birth – as their happiest.

I'm afraid that some of the men who read this are already beginning to realize the dreadful message this piece of data carries. Yes, sirs, that's the truth. None of you, my dear brothers, featured in the happiest moment of your wife's life! (To cheer you up a bit, let me tell you that you do feature in the happiest moment of your mother's life. Feeling better?)

Man is for woman a means: the purpose is always the child.

Friedrich Nietzsche

A Bad Guess
After conducting that survey, I conducted another, supportive survey in which I asked men to guess what their wives' happiest moment might be. This survey revealed that men are very wise and know many things, but are quite the idiots when it comes to their leading ladies. Here's a typical selection of answers:

The first time my wife saw me

The first time I hugged my wife

The moment I proposed (*In fact, this incident did feature as first choice here and there in the women's answers, but it was nowhere near the moment of giving birth. The actual wedding was very often ranked at number 3, 4 or 5.*)

The first time we kissed

The moment my wife realized she wanted to spend the rest of her life with me

Whenever I lecture about the things that men think women choose as their peak moments in life, the women in the audience react with loud and uncontrollable laughter, while the men don't even get the joke.

> Only two things are infinite, the universe and human stupidity, and I'm not sure about the former.
>
> Albert Einstein

An Unrepresentative but Important Sample

After reading the results of my survey, I decided to ask my wife about her happiest moment. Driving home, I thought deeply about the method I should use. How could I pop the question so that the answer wouldn't disappoint me? Sitting at the kitchen table, I turned to my wife and said: 'My dear, I've been conducting a survey recently on people's moments of greatest happiness, and it has produced the oddest and most illogical result. Many of the surveyed women made no sense at all and merely wrote that their happiest moment was when they gave birth to a child. I very much hope that this is not what you would say. Thank you in advance for your candid reply.'

My wife answered boldly, filling my heart with pride. 'The moment of giving birth?' she said. 'Not at all.' I almost grew taller with pride. After giving it another moment's thought, my wife added, 'It is not the moment of birth. Giving birth is messy and painful. It is … the moment right *after* giving birth.'

Men, Women and Insurance Policies

Here's another, somewhat related story. Many years ago I spoke before the chief executives of a major insurance company, and told them what women had chosen as their moments of ultimate joy. One of the managers raised his hand, looking very excited, and before he was even given permission to speak said that he had to tell us something. 'Go ahead, if you have to,' I responded.

He then explained that, according to surveys his insurance company had conducted, when men buy life insurance they almost always make the beneficiary their wife (I myself had in fact done the same thing); but when women take out a life insurance policy, they very often name their children as beneficiaries (this will come as no surprise to my female readers, but as a typical male I know that this fact took us all completely by surprise).

The insurance company, deciding to study this dry fact a little further, asked their female clients to explain why they decided to leave everything to their children.

The common answer (which I've modified slightly for reading purposes) was this: 'Of course, my children should get the money when I die. Of course, I'll leave nothing to my husband. He will most certainly remarry, and I wouldn't have my insurance benefits land in the hands of his second wife, not even by accident.'

This argument gave rise to two interesting questions. The first has to do with the fact that most women outlive their husbands – so why are they worrying about the substitute wife?

The second question is associated with the fact that very few men even considered the possibility of their wife's second husband. Why is that? My guess is that it has to do with the aforementioned male idiocy. So many men believe they are so wonderful, so special, so impossible to imitate (not to mention exceed), that they don't even consider that their widows might remarry.

How can they marry someone else after living with me?

What many men wonder

I married a man who was quite inferior. Most women do.

Confession of a married woman

Well, now the time has come to introduce you to the happiest moments of men. I believe that once we've learned what makes the stronger and less fair gender happy, we'll understand why women are right to leave their insurance money to their children. It's simply because children are not as infantile as some grown men.

What Makes Men Happy? (Male Psychology, or 'Joe Meets Penélope Cruz')

Freud may have been unable to uncover women's deepest and most secret desires, but he clearly knew a lot about the desires of men. Others did too. Czech novelist Milan Kundera, for example, feels that a course in male psychology shouldn't take more than two minutes. He believes men have two major desires. The desire you think is first actually comes second; while their first, truest, deepest, most sincere desire is (Kundera thinks) to be viewed as great sinners.

When I first read about Kundera's views, I doubted their validity, but with time I've become increasingly convinced that he's right. Let me prove this thesis with an example of your average Joe.

Suppose Joe is presented with two options to choose from. In the first, he can spend a night with Penélope Cruz, Beyoncé Giselle Knowles-Carter and Adriana Lima. In this option, he would have no proof of that night and no one will ever believe him (except for his favourite shrink, who might prescribe some pills). In the second option, Joe will stay home alone all night, but receive a notary-authenticated document that reads:

Dear Joe,
> *Thank you for a wonderful night.*
> *We've never met a man like you, and probably never will.*
> *Forever your lovers and admirers,*

Penélope, Beyoncé and Adriana

If you know Joe, you know exactly what he would choose.

Kundera's insight became even more evidently accurate in my survey. Many men, whose answers were unsigned, could not let go of their desire to make an impression and be viewed as great sinners. Many of those wonderful moments that men described – incidentally, men of all ages – could not get past the censorship bureau of this book. Their moments comprised: sex, sex and more sex.

What about the moments of birth? How many men feel that the births of their children were their happiest moments?

The answer from my survey is: 14 per cent. That's the ratio of men who said that the birth of their child was the happiest moment of their lives.

When I mentioned this figure in one of my lectures, a man rose from the audience and said it didn't sound right because that figure was much larger than he'd expected. He argued that most men actually referred to their own appearance on Earth, and asked me to review the answers again to see if he was right.

The truth is that I never anticipated that option in the first place, and thus my survey was incomplete. I double-checked the answers the men had given me and discovered that while some men explicitly referred to 'my son's birth', 'when my daughter was born' or 'the first time I saw my twins', others wrote 'the moment of birth' – and I'll never know what they meant.

Of course, men mentioned all the regular moments of joy: 'I graduated with honours', 'the moment I first met my wife', 'skydiving', 'riding my bike on the Dead Sea slopes', 'the first time I saw a woman naked', 'the day I made peace with my dad after years of silence', 'the day I became a CEO', and so on. You must have noticed that these moments of happiness are quite similar to the moments that younger women mentioned, those who hadn't yet had children, but still it seems that men's moments of joy are often strange (or is it just me?).

Instead of listing all of those moments, let me tell you about one that explains and clarifies them all.

The Great Scorer

One day I was invited to speak at a gathering held in honour of an important person. Since it was a special occasion, I did something I never do and brought props with me – in this case the (censored) notes describing the happiest moments of men. When I reached the point in which I usually tell my audience about these moments, I decided to pull out a few notes and read each one out loud.

I pulled out the first note.

'The happiest moment of my life,' one of my male respondents wrote, 'was when Uri Malmilian of Beitar Jerusalem scored the second goal in the cup final of 1974, and Beitar beat Maccabi Tel Aviv 2:1 and won the cup!'

I was about to tell everyone how sad and pathetic this happy moment was (I mean, has this really been the happiest moment of his life? He didn't even score the goal – Malmilian did!) when the strangest thing happened.

The guest of honour jumped up from his chair and yelled: 'The man is wrong! That goal was scored in 1976, not 1974, and it's the happiest moment of my life too! Oh, it was simply amazing,' he fervently exclaimed.

'A few minutes earlier,' he continued, 'when the game was tied, that same Malmilian had missed a penalty kick. He paid his debt with interest when he scored that goal from an impossible angle. Malmilian was elected "player of the season" that year and Beitar finished second in the league.' (He went on and on about that wondrous occasion, but I don't want to bore my readers who are not football, or Beitar, fans.)

> Some people believe football is a matter of life and death.
> I am very disappointed with that attitude. I can assure you it
> is much, much more important than that.
>
> Bill Shankly, former manager of Liverpool

That's just wonderful, I thought. What exactly was I supposed to do now? Generally speaking, I prefer to get paid for lectures I give, and I knew that downplaying the happiest moment of the guest of honour would not close the deal. I therefore decided that this was an opportune moment for me to try out my improvisation skills. In other words, I lied.

But nothing is that simple on our complicated planet. What ended up happening was that the lie I came up with then is one of my firmest beliefs today.

The Happiest Moment

'Look how wonderful it is,' I told the celebrants, 'that we men can find such moments of joy in such small things' (though I'm not sure football qualified in their minds as such a 'small thing').

'This means that we're closer than women to Pooh's philosophy of life. Pooh is happy with anything that happens to him. He comes up with silly poems and loves them. He uses a balloon to fly, which is great fun too. The ability to categorize small things as moments of joy is an art form.'

When I reviewed the answers women gave in this survey I realized that, with very few exceptions (notably the student who said that her greatest moment of joy was when her cat recovered), women do not play small when it comes to their private happiness. They need grand things as raw material which they can process into joyous moments: a birth, a symphony orchestra conducted by Gustavo Dudamel, a trip around the world that includes a cruise through icebergs, or a huge wedding.

Personal and Sacred

One day, as I finished lecturing about the issues this book is dealing with, a lady came up to me and said she was my student several years back, took a course in statistics, and that as an expert in statistics I should be aware of the fact that very often the answers both men and women give pollsters are not necessarily the truth. She has two children and a career that is not less important, she said, adding that she does not need great and mighty things to feel happy. Yet, she confessed, she believed that if she were polled on this, she would probably give the ordinary answers people give. That was a very interesting point. As an expert on statistical issues, I am fully aware of the fact that sometimes people answer pollsters as they believe they are expected to: men state that their football teams thrill them the most, while women speak of giving birth or getting married as the happiest moments of their lives. This does not mean it is the absolute truth.

When I came home that evening, I shared my thoughts with my wife and asked about her view of this. Instead of answering, Daniela (we've been married more than a quarter of a century and been together since the beginning of time) asked me about my happiest moment. I said I needed to think about it a little. After giving it much thought (a little wasn't enough), I told her that if I ignored all the dramatic events, my happiest moments take place almost every morning, when we sip our coffees, read the paper, and chat. Then I added that mornings in which we drink our coffees in silence are not less happy.

And would you tell that to an unknown pollster? Daniela asked.

Probably not, I said. For many people, it would seem, their happiest moments are personal and sacred. They would not easily confide it to some strange pollster who conducts strange polls.

In the Beginning

The only joy in the world is to begin.

Cesare Pavese

I believe that a beginning, as lame as it may be, is better than the happiest ending. But we should also remember this:

Every new beginning comes from some other beginning's end.

Seneca

Indeed, we must remember that an ending is also an opportunity for a new beginning.

Before we move on to something really important, I suggest we all take a break, rest a little, do nothing for an hour or two, and munch on a little something.

A Page that Really Matters

Here's an idea that can help settle many conflicts and contradictions in our lives and minds. To the best of my knowledge the originator of this idea is the German writer Thomas Mann, and physicist Niels Bohr expanded on it, arguing that it was one of the wisest and deepest ideas he ever heard:

> There are trivial truths and profound truths. The opposite of a trivial truth is plainly false. The opposite of a profound truth is a profound truth.

Here's a small example to help us grasp this concept. When we state that 'two and two make four', we're expressing a 'trivial' truth, because if we'd argued the opposite and claimed that two and two did not make four, we'd be talking nonsense.

Referring to the second part of the idea above, I would say: 'Life is a miracle, the most wonderful thing imaginable.' Now, this is profound truth, but it is just as true as 'Life is misery: a futile interruption of the blessed peace of nothingness' (paraphrasing pessimist German philosopher Arthur Schopenhauer).

We'll explore this topic later.

I have a little confession to make. If I were to go back to academic research, I would perhaps undertake the study of emotions. While everyone agrees that emotions are central in our lives, they remain a fascinating subject about which very little is known.

2.

Emotions and Desires

> Let's not forget that the little emotions are the great captains
> of our lives and we obey them without realizing it.
>
> Vincent Van Gogh

Homo sentiens (Feeling/Emotional Man) sounds just as good as *Homo sapiens* (Thinking/Wise Man). Quite surprisingly, however, scientists disagree on the answer to a seemingly basic question: what are emotions? Because it's easy to pose hard questions, let me throw in a few of my own. What is the difference between emotion and feeling? Can emotions be consciously awakened or redirected? Can emotions be described neurologically? What is the impact of culture on emotions, and are certain emotions found in given cultures while others are not? Can we say that animals have human-like emotions, or are humans alone in experiencing emotions? How many emotions can one experience simultaneously?

Let us build a table of emotions, acknowledging immediately that the following table (overleaf) is neither exhaustive, nor scientific, nor binding.

I've left a few boxes for you to fill in at will. Furthermore, although I created this table quite spontaneously and with no specific method in mind, I did try to avoid repetition. For example, mercy and compassion are two different emotions: mercy comes from above (God has mercy), but compassion exists at eye level.

Let's conduct a little experiment. Think about your own repertoire of emotions: which are the most frequent and which are rare? If you enjoy working with numbers, rank them by percentage points that measure the relative duration of each emotion when it appears. The total doesn't have to add up to 100 per cent, because we can have several emotions at the same time. I believe that if I collected my readers' results, I'd discover substantial differences between people.

Now let's repeat this experiment with a slight modification. This time, list the emotions you would like to keep and those you would love to give up.

A serious analysis of every emotion that exists would probably require writing a few thick volumes, which is why for the purposes of this chapter I've decided to focus on only four emotions: Anger, Envy, Pride and Joy. We shall examine Anger first (so as not to upset anyone).

Have you ever noticed the looks on the faces of sports players who have just scored a goal or jump-shot a three-pointer? Many raise their fists in the air in a threatening motion and make a frightening face, or scream, or clench their teeth. You'd expect them to be very happy, but instead they look mad as hell. What is that? It seems to me, and some psychologists agree, that men are generally 'allowed' to express every emotion they have in just a single way: anger. They look angry when they are happy or sad, elated or desperate … and, of course, when they are angry. Recently I've noticed that, while fighting for equality, women too tend to express rage and anger more often than we've seen them do before. Perhaps displaying anger externally eliminates inward-turning anger and rage (that is, depression), which is a good thing. Or is it?

Are you an angry person? Do you tend to explode with anger? And if so, would you like to rid yourself of that emotion?

Ralph Waldo Emerson said that different people boil at different temperatures. Some people cannot be shaken out of their calm, while others become furious even before they know why.

> Be not hasty in thy spirit to be angry, for anger rests in the bosom of fools.
>
> Ecclesiastes 7:9

I must agree with King Solomon (who is traditionally viewed as the author of Ecclesiastes), because I've seen anger turn people into fools. I'm also aware of the clever advice of counting to ten (or even 77) before I react angrily. Clearly, anger is characteristic of fools who cannot and have no

Happiness	Sadness	Anger	
Disappointment	Love	Mercy	
Hunger	Curiosity	Confusion	
Lust	Frustration	Fondness	
Joy	Confidence	Disdain	
Despair	Worry	Hostility	
Loathing	Compassion	Shame	

Happiness and Other Small Things of Absolute Importance

Rage	Shame	Envy	Jealousy
Sorrow	Boredom	Amazement	Gratitude
Pride	Hope	Horror	Remorse
Disgust	Indifference	Gloating	Relief
Depression	Agitation	Longing	Nostalgia
Euphoria	Grief	Inner peace	Emptiness
Frustration	Loneliness	Anxiety	

desire to get the other side of the story. Even when I'm sure I'm right, I know that being angry is punishing myself for the stupidity of others (remember the Taxi Driver story?).

So I know. Is that knowledge helpful? Well, sometimes it is and sometimes it isn't.

Though I know all there is to know about the direct and indirect, internal and external damage that anger causes, I still get mad. Giving ourselves sound advice is easy; following it is a different story. The truth is that emotions play a major part in our lives, often a much larger part than reason.

Of course, things are always more complicated than they seem at first or even second glance.

My wife, a chemical engineer by profession, has reached an important understanding. In nature, she told me, each substance has a typical, unique and fixed boiling point. We can artificially change it, however, by using other substances that act as inhibitors, thereby raising the boiling point. For example, anyone who cooks knows that salted water takes longer to boil than water alone. The same applies to people. Their boiling points can be raised. Wisdom can be salt for our water, since it's supposed to improve the way we react in given situations and help us act consciously, from a more balanced, rational and adult place.

Yet we must remember that even salted, it is only *slightly* modified water. By the same token, people who gain wisdom remain quite the same, only a little wiser.

Perhaps anger is unavoidable? Maybe those who stop feeling angry or never get mad are no longer human? I tend to believe that people who cannot feel anger have fallen into the deadening realm of indifference, where caring doesn't exist. After all, there are things in this world that must upset us, things we must resist or rage against, simply because we are human.

> If you are neutral in situations of injustice, you have chosen
> the side of the oppressor.
>
> Bishop Desmond Tutu

Further, I believe that just as each of us has his or her own anger threshold, we experience other emotions in varying degrees too. Some people have hearts full of compassion, while others never feel sorry for anyone. Some people worry constantly, troubled even by the fact that the universe keeps expanding, while others only begin to worry a little when their parachute doesn't open after a minute of free-falling. Some people follow their desires at the first whim, while others rarely desire anything.

Similarly, certain people are always sad. They are saddened when they hear the rain falling outside their window, when there's not enough rain, or when a pimple appears on their nose. The musician Franz Schubert was so deeply melancholic that he prayed every night that he'd never see daylight again. On the other hand, certain people experience sadness only in the face of huge tragedies, while others are very rarely sad.

They say that the American poet Walt Whitman was never sad and loved everyone and everything. Was he inhuman? While King Solomon felt that 'all is vanity', Whitman believed there was 'nothing else but miracles' and wrote one of my ten favourite poems of all time:

Miracles

Why! who makes much of a miracle?
As to me, I know of nothing else but miracles
Whether I walk the streets of Manhattan,
Or dart my sight over the roofs of houses toward the sky,
Or wade with naked feet along the beach, just in the edge of the water
Or stand under trees in the woods
Or talk by day with any one I love – or sleep in the bed at night with
any one I love,

Or sit at table at dinner with the rest

Or look at strangers opposite me riding in the car

Or watch honey-bees busy around the hive, of a summer forenoon,

Or animals feeding in the fields,

Or birds – or the wonderfulness of insects in the air

*Or the wonderfulness of the sun-down – or of stars shining so quiet
and bright*

Or the exquisite, delicate, thin curve of the new moon in spring

*Or whether I go among those I like best, and that like me best –
mechanics, boatmen, farmers*

Or among the savants – or to the soiree – or to the opera

Or stand a long while looking at the movements of machinery

Or behold children at their sports

*Or the admirable sight of the perfect old man, or the perfect old
woman*

Or the sick in hospitals, or the dead carried to burial,

Or my own eyes and figure in the glass

These, with the rest, one and all, are to me miracles

The whole referring – yet each distinct, and in its place.

To me, every hour of the light and dark is a miracle

Every cubic inch of space is a miracle

Every square yard of the surface of the earth is spread with the same,

Every foot of the interior swarms with the same

*Every spear of grass – the frames, limbs, organs, of men and women
and all that concerns them,*

All these to me are unspeakably perfect miracles.

*To me the sea is a continual miracle; the fishes that swim – the rocks
– the motion of the waves – the shipswith men in them,*

What stranger miracles are there?

Walt Whitman

As much as I admire the quality of finding good in everything, I cannot understand how anyone can love all of humanity. I feel that many of those who declare that they do, actually hate people. Dostoevsky believed that it's much easier to have an abstract love for mankind than to love a real person. Personally, I often identify with the wonderful Polish poet Wisława Szymborska (Nobel laureate), who wrote:

I prefer myself loving people to myself loving mankind.

Freud believed love is finite and we should think carefully before giving ours to others. If that's the case, should we really give our love to lilac flowers or blades of grass? Whitman felt we should. The great American poet was kind and full of love. He even believed that all things are perfect – good or bad. Flowers, caterpillars, a thunderstorm, the genitals, every old or young man and woman, health, sickness, life and death – they are all divine and splendid, and all is wonderfully well in this world.

So, we started out discussing anger, and ended up speaking about love. That's a good transition.

***

Now, let's speak about Envy.

Envy was the cause of the first homicide in human history, at least according to the Bible. Envy, a pleasureless sin, is one of the Seven Deadly Sins of Christianity (the other six being wrath, greed, sloth, pride, lust, and gluttony – as presented by Pope Gregory I, who decided to play the role of the Mendeleev of sins and formed their canonic table).

People really don't need much to live – just food, clothing and a roof over their heads. Everything else they own is meant to match the tastes of others, and mainly to 'out-rich' them and inspire envy.

Comparison is the thief of joy.

Anonymous

Never keep up with the Joneses. Drag them down to your
level. It's cheaper.

Quentin Crisp

Envy is one of the most fascinating psychological phenomena. People
envy the status, abilities, wealth and experiences of others. We envy
anything, even a splendid funeral. At the same time, almost all of us also
want to *be* envied.

People are willing to do quite a lot to be loved, and
everything to be envied.

François de La Rochefoucauld

King Solomon tried to ease the envious mind, saying:

I have seen servants upon horses, and princes walking as
servants upon the earth.

Ecclesiastes 10:7

Life is fickle indeed, and what goes up must come down, as we know. If
there's one thing that's permanent in this world, it's change. As we've all
had cause to realize, life is what happens when we're busy making other
plans, and no one knows what tomorrow will bring. I'm sure God laughs
His head off whenever He listens to our plans.

Now, it's a fact that envy lasts longer than the happiness we envied in
the first place. This is one of the reasons why envy is not worth it. We don't
know what might happen and to whom, and there's no pleasure in envy, as
it clearly makes those experiencing it suffer.

Although we might know all that, my advice is scarcely worth the paper it's
written on. It's easy to tell people not to envy, and to present solid evidence and
ironclad logic against it, but it's almost impossible to prevent envy in practice.

Do you know anyone who never envies? I don't. We're all slaves to the green-eyed monster, each at his own level. As an example, take the following story, for which I once put pen to paper:

The Lake and the Fountain

The silent lake spent years watching the magnificent fountain they placed on its shores, and greatly envied the pretty shapes it created and the sounds it produced daily. 'So full of life it is. So lively. It never rests or tires. Never misses a moment of life. How I yearn to be a fountain,' the lake thought. 'I wish I could live its interesting life. How often have I heard people cheer and laugh at its water tricks? When they reach my shores, they just walk past me in silence. Sometimes there are couples that stand there holding hands, for reasons I cannot understand. Others just sit on the grass or a bench, looking bored at the static and uniform display I put on. I wish I were a fountain, but sadly I am a lake and even as a lake I am nothing special. I am neither deep, nor big or beautiful. I am so plain.'

The fountain spent years watching the clear and silent lake, and envied it immensely. 'How calm it is. Look at it: it is not trying to impress anyone and its waters rush nowhere. They definitely need no acrobatics. As for me, I am addicted to people's attention,' the fountain thought. 'I will do anything to make them marvel at my performance, but I am weary. Oh, how happy is the lake. People just stroll around it and it does not have to entertain them. They sit on its banks and enjoy the quiet splashing sounds of its tiny waves. That lake has it so very easy. If I stopped making these shapes, no one would visit me: nothing is more pathetic than a silent and static fountain. How I yearn to be a silent lake. I'd give anything to switch places, if only for a little while.'

Though it may be concealed, there's a strong connection between envy and friendship. Here, *The Little Prince* can educate us. Near the end of Chapter 4, Saint-Exupéry wrote one of the book's most famous lines:

To forget a friend is sad. Not everyone has had a friend.

When I first read *The Little Prince* at the age of 12, that sentence surprised me. What did he mean by 'Not everyone has had a friend'? I didn't have many, but I knew for certain that most people have lots of friends. What's the big deal about losing one? I couldn't understand Saint-Exupéry at all.

Years later, when I was a mathematics student at Tel Aviv University, the local bookstore was one of my favourite spots. Since my apartment (not to mention my budget) was too small for all the books I wanted, I used to read entire sections of books right there, and only if I really loved a book would I buy it.

One day, I came across *Pensées* by Blaise Pascal. I opened a page and what did I find?

Men deceive and flatter each other. No one speaks of us in our presence as he does of us in our absence. Human society is founded on mutual deceit; few friendships would endure if each knew what his friend said of him in his absence.

I set it down as a fact that if all men knew what each said of the other, there would not be four friends in the world.

Blaise Pascal, *Pensées* 100 and 101

It's amazing how pessimistic that is. (By the way, I can cite the numbers of individual Pensées without reference to the Internet, as I eventually bought that book.)

When I read these thoughts, they reminded me of *The Little Prince*. I had to wonder: perhaps the two Frenchmen are right and I am wrong? Or perhaps only Frenchmen think this way?

Well, as it happens other nationals share the belief that a true friend is a rarity. Ralph Waldo Emerson said, 'A *friend* may well be reckoned the masterpiece of nature,' and he was an American. The Chinese philosopher Mencius believed that 'A true friend is one soul in two people,' and Aristotle agreed, and he was Greek. Still, the great Greek sage made the following exclamation too:

O friends, there are no friends at all!

At that point, I started suspecting that I was missing something, and that a friend is indeed a precious and rare thing to have. It took a few more years before I understood what was happening.

The problem starts with the definition of 'friend'. People say, 'A friend in need is a friend indeed.' Well, a proverb does not become true just because it rhymes. Many words rhyme with 'need' and 'indeed' – greed, agreed, misdeed, lead, bead, speed, reed, shahid and hasid* – but that doesn't mean a thing.

I decided to consult another Frenchman, and after I read his cynical words, visiting a sick friend was never the same again:

How nice it is to visit a friend in hospital. You know at once that you are in a much better shape than he is.

Channelling François de La Rochefoucauld

This brought me to the following conclusion. When you feel bad, sick or sad ... you'd better keep it to yourself. Knowing that was the case would make your enemies happy and your friends sad, and I want to do neither.

Of course, I'd never put down people who get me through bad times, but to me one of the most important qualities a friend should have is the inclination to stick around when times are good. The fact is that when we're doing really well, we start losing friends. I do not count fake friends that stick

---

* These last two are martyr (Arabic) and devotee (Hebrew/Yiddish) respectively.

around for the sake of kudos, or the possibility that they'll benefit in some way.

In any event, it's very hard to tame the green-eyed monster.

Spinoza noted the interesting fact that we only envy people comparable to us. No philosophy professor ever envies Spinoza, unless he lost his mind and hasn't found it yet. It's more likely for him to envy a colleague, another philosophy professor who is slightly more successful or even a little wiser. It's no accident that the first recorded murder in human history was a fratricide. We don't envy an oak tree for its height nor a lion for its might. Similarly, we don't envy people who have slipped away from this world and moved on to greener pastures. They are no longer our peers (it's very easy for me to praise a writer who is no longer with us).

Little Women (a short, non-existent play)

Jane, 60, is alone at home. Mary, her friend of the same age, comes calling. Mary knocks on the door.

Jane: Who is it?

Mary: It's me. Mary. Open quickly. I've great news to tell you.

Jane opens the door and Mary bursts in, breathing heavily.

Mary: You won't believe it when I tell you what happened.

Jane: What happened?

Mary: Don't ask. (*Actually meaning, 'Please ask. I can't wait to tell you.'*)

Jane: Won't you sit down?

Mary: I can't. Listen, I just won $12 million in the lottery!

Jane: Oh, that's wonderful (*mildly excited*).

Mary: Wait. That's not all! As soon as I got the lottery call, my youngest called to tell me that he graduated in his PhD studies with honours!

Jane: Maz'l Tof! (*barely pleased*)

Mary: There's more. Before I had time to congratulate my boy, my husband came in and told me he's a Nobel Prize candidate. How about them apples, huh?

Jane: Oh, I'm very happy for you (*all traces of happiness are gone*).

Mary: Oy, I forgot to tell you, I'm so excited. My daughter Laurie has been proposed to by the Prince of Transylvania. They'll have a royal wedding in the summer!

Jane tries to say something, but chokes. There's only so much she can take.

Curtain.

***

True friendship should meet at least two requirements:

The ability to rejoice in your friend's happiness

The willingness to do things that may not benefit you, but will benefit your friend.

These are necessary conditions, but they are not sufficient in themselves. In any event, few friends meet even these two criteria.

> Shared joys make a friend, not shared sufferings.
>
> Friedrich Nietzsche

> A true friend is the greatest of all blessings, and that which we take the least care of all to acquire.
>
> François de la Rochefoucauld

Envy and anger are two of the greatest obstacles we need to overcome before we can experience joy. To discuss this joyous issue, I'd like to turn to one of the biggest experts in this field, St Francis of Assisi.

This Christian saint was born in the late 12th century as the son of a wealthy merchant. Upon having a revelation (or a few, depending on your source), he decided to renounce all earthly possessions (a biography that resembles that of Siddhartha Gautama Buddha, founder of Buddhism), and embraced Joy and Jesus. St Francis was deeply influenced by Matthew 10:9–10, which reads: 'Provide neither gold, nor silver, nor brass in your purses, nor scrip for your journey, neither two coats, neither shoes, nor yet staves ...' (This always reminds me of the splendid scene in Fellini's movie *Roma* where he mocks the Vatican clergy who put on a splendid 'fashion show' and display of riches, clearly having forgotten all about either Matthew or Francis.)

Two orders, one for men and one for women, were established in Francis's spirit. St Francis of Assisi was named patron saint of animals and also, together with Catherine of Siena, patron saint of Italy. His followers lived a simple and austere life indeed, happily wandering around Umbria and singing songs of praise for almost anything.

Many legends are associated with St Francis, who reportedly used to talk to animals, flowers and trees as if they were his friends. According to one legend, he persuaded a wolf to forgo his evil ways and even convinced the creature to make a peace pact with the local villagers. Another legend has him thanking his donkey for its faithful services, which made the donkey burst into tears.

For it is in giving that we receive and it is in pardoning that we are pardoned.

St Francis of Assisi

Scholars consider St Francis the first Italian poet known today. Many writers and thinkers were influenced by his lore. Here is one of my favourite tales, as told by Tolstoy:

Perfect Joy

One winter day, St Francis was returning to his monastery from Perugia with Brother Leo, and the bitter cold made them shiver. St Francis called to Brother Leo, who was walking a bit ahead of him, and said: 'Brother Leo, even if the Friars Minor [Conventual Franciscans] in every country give a great example of holiness and integrity and good edification – nevertheless, write down and note carefully that perfect joy is not in that.'

And when he had walked on a bit, St Francis called him again, saying: 'Brother Leo, even if one of the Friars Minor gives sight to the blind, heals the paralyzed, drives out devils, gives hearing back to the deaf, makes the lame walk, and restores speech to the dumb, and what is still more, brings back to life a man who has been dead four days – write that perfect joy is not in that.'

And going on a bit, St Francis cried out again in a strong voice: 'Brother Leo, if a Friar Minor knew all languages and all sciences and Scripture, if he also knew how to prophesy and to reveal not only the future but also the secrets of the consciences and minds of others – write down and note carefully that perfect joy is not in that.'

And as they walked on, after a while St Francis called again forcefully: 'Brother Leo, Little Lamb of God, even if a Friar Minor could speak with the voice of an angel, and knew the courses of the stars and the powers of herbs, and knew all about the treasures in the earth, and if he knew the qualities of birds and fishes, animals, humans, roots, trees, rocks and waters – write down and note carefully that true joy is not in that.'

Now when he had been talking this way, Brother Leo in great amazement asked him: 'Father, I beg you in God's name to tell me where perfect joy is.'

And St Francis replied: 'When we come to St Mary of the Angels, soaked by the rain and frozen by the cold, all soiled with mud and suffering from hunger, and we ring at the gate of our own monastery, and the brother porter comes and says angrily: 'Who are you?' And we say: 'We are two of your brothers.' And he contradicts us, saying: 'You are not telling the truth.

Rather you are two rascals who go around deceiving people and stealing what they give to the poor. Go away!' And he does not open for us, but makes us stand outside in the snow and rain, cold and hungry, until night falls – then, if we endure all those insults and cruel rebuffs patiently without being troubled and without complaining, and if we reflect humbly and charitably that God makes him speak against us, oh, Brother Leo, write that perfect joy is there!

'And if we continue to knock, and the porter comes out in anger, and drives us away with curses and hard blows like bothersome scoundrels, saying: 'Get away from here, you dirty thieves! Go to the hospital! Who do you think you are? You certainly won't eat or sleep here.' And if we bear it patiently and take the insults with joy and love in our hearts, oh, Brother Leo, that is perfect joy!'

Things My Mother Told Me (or, the Polygraph Test)

My mother was a teacher of Russian literature for many years, and though she has been an Israeli for the past few decades she still enjoys and admires Russian culture. One day, while visiting me, she related the following story:

A week ago I was watching Russian TV and stumbled upon a show of the kind you don't like, a game show. This one was called The Polygraph. Participants are hooked up to a lie detector and asked increasingly embarrassing questions. When the machine confirms they spoke the truth, they win money and the sum grows until they answer some 20 questions truthfully and they receive the accumulated sum, or – if the machine decides they lied – they lose it all.

A woman who competed on the show did very well and had a large sum of money to her credit when the hosts presented her with a relatively simple question that was not embarrassing at all:

'Are you happy?' The woman said she was, but the machine said she wasn't. She lost everything, and the network sponsors kept their money.'

What happened there? Clearly, if the contestant was aware she wasn't in seventh heaven and overflowing with bliss and joy, she could have admitted as much and walked away with the jackpot. There's no shame in being unhappy. So why did she not admit that? It seems to me that she truly believed that, given the circumstances, she was happy, and she said so.

Though I'm fully aware of the limitations of a lie detector, I thought it might be very interesting to see how the machine would respond if we hooked up several people and asked them if they were happy. Particularly interesting would be cases in which people thought they were not happy, and the polygraph disagreed.

As I've been writing this, I've decided I'll subject myself to such a test, but only after I finish writing this book. I am too happy now and don't want some silly machine to spoil it for me.

On Pride and Prejudice

Once, the Little Prince encountered the conceited man.

> 'Ah! Ah! I am about to receive a visit from an admirer!'
> he exclaimed from afar, when he first saw the Little Prince
> coming. For to conceited men, all other men are admirers.
>
> Antoine de Saint-Exupéry, *The Little Prince*

'A proud look' is 'the first of seven abominations' listed in Proverbs 6, and Christians traditionally place pride among the seven deadly sins. So, what is pride?

Spinoza maintained that a person is proud when, out of self-love, he thinks he is more than he really is. If Spinoza asked me, I would say that pride is an over-motivated error of judgement. In any event, Spinoza remarked that the opposite doesn't exist, that no man thinks of himself to be less than he is out of self-hate.

> He who despises himself, esteems himself as a self-despiser.
>
> Fyodor Dostoevsky and Friedrich Nietzsche
> (if they ever decided to coin phrases together)

Judging from my experience, I would add that when a person says bad things about himself, he is actually fishing for compliments, praise and encouragement. On certain occasions I perform in front of an audience, playing the piano. Before I started my recitals, I used to tell my would-be listeners that piano playing is not my main line of work, that actually I'm a mathematician and a writer. Having made that statement, I used to feel most encouraged, knowing that it wouldn't be terrible if I slipped up here and there. I stopped doing that recently. If you can't play well, don't play in front of an audience. It's perfectly all right, of course, to play in the privacy of your own home where only you and your non-judgemental neighbours can hear.

The title of this subsection is no accident. Jane Austen was indeed an expert on pride. (When I was younger I used to ridicule her writing, but that was because I was arrogant and stupid. Today I very much enjoy reading the works of this wonderful writer.) Just look at the distinctions she makes between the various types of pride:

> Vanity and pride are different things.[…] A person may be proud without being vain. Pride relates more to our opinion of ourselves; vanity to what we would have others think of us.
>
> Jane Austen, *Pride and Prejudice*

What lovely insight! Though *superbia* (the Latin name of that sin) is translated into 'vanity' and 'pride' interchangeably, these are two different things.

Inspired by wise Austen, I should like to add that I believe that modesty and humility are also two different things. A person who is truly humble demonstrates perhaps the rarest and most beautiful of human qualities. Modesty, however, is often a kind of pride in disguise. For example, I once read an interview with a chess world champion (whom I shall not name) in which he was asked how he manages to see so many moves in advance. 'I am an ordinary man,' the champ said. 'There is nothing special about me.' And I wondered: why this answer? If he is an ordinary man, than the rest of us are plain morons. I don't believe he did not know that he'd been blessed with a special gift. An honest answer would have been: 'I am a chess mastermind, and therefore I can see the next few moves before they take place.' What's the point of the fake modesty in his actual answer?

When tennis champion Roger Federer was in his prime, he used to offer enlightening explanations when he lost games, which was very rare at the time. He would say: 'I lost today because I did not concentrate enough. Clearly, I am the world's best tennis player, and when I am in the zone, no one can beat me.' I'd take this honest and proud answer over any kind of fake modesty any time.

Considering the psychology of modesty, we can detect an interesting dynamic here. Why would people pretend to be modest? Possibly because they think that if they told us what they really think of themselves, we'd be so amazed that we'd lose control of how we might respond. I'd say to him: 'Don't worry. We're cool.'

Don't be so modest; you're not that great.

Golda Meir

Three Is Cacophony
Two important rabbis were praying in the woods together when one rabbi

fell to the ground and yelled: 'I am nothing. I am a big zero. My body is a walking wound with nine holes. I have a sinner's soul. I am not worthy!'

The other rabbi hurled himself down, mumbling a very similar sentiment: 'I am no more than a bug. My life is worth nothing at all.'

While the two rabbis were squirming on the ground, they suddenly saw a young yeshiva student hitting the ground next to them, yelling: 'I am nothing! God, I am less than nothing. A little bug is huge next to me!'

The two rabbis stood up, grabbed the youngster by the collar, looked down upon him, and said: 'Listen, you arrogant boy! Who are you to say you are nothing?'

A conceited man, even if he spends a long time close to a wise man, shall not know the taste of wisdom more than a spoon knows the taste of food it conveys.

Leo Tolstoy

A Very Short Treatise on Desire

Lord, grant that I may always desire more than I can accomplish.

Michelangelo

We all have passions and desires, and they vary. To love, to see, to hear and to talk are but a drop in the ocean of human desires. Spinoza believed that passion (*cupiditas*) is the core of man's essence, but he also said:

Man's inability to control his passions is what I call enslavement, because a person who is subject to them no longer holds his own ground, and against his will is attracted to evil, though he can clearly see good before him.

Baruch Spinoza, *Ethics*

Spinoza truly believed not only that the thinking mind is unable to overcome passions, but that the two are not even of equal power. Passions can be defeated only by stronger passions. While Oscar Wilde thought that the only way to get rid of temptation is to yield to it, Spinoza tells us that the only way to get rid of temptation is to find a stronger one.

Before we start dwelling on the subject, let us first make an important distinction between desire, demand and need – and discuss their interactions. In his *La Signification du Phallus*, Jacques Lacan, the prominent and highly influential French psychoanalyst and philosopher of psychiatry, made the following important distinction, which he presented in mathematical form:

$$Desire = Demand - Need$$

That is, if we subtract what we need from what we demand, what's left is desire. In most cases, a need is a biological urge or instinct, and we express it by demanding things. What we have left after the original need was satisfied is the result of desire. Lacan added that desire is also active along margins where demand is not directly related to need.

Here are a few small examples. If a person needs four pairs of shoes for his everyday life, but has 707 pairs in his closet, the remaining 703 pairs represent his desire for shoes. When at a dinner party or family gathering we keep eating, even though we have satisfied our physical hunger, this is gluttony or a desire for food.

In my private library I have more books than I could possibly read in a lifetime. Here, there was no biological need. This is the result of my desire for the written word. When there's no biological need, demand and desire are fused together. I refer to such cases as 'pure desire'.

A need appears in the face of an object that can satisfy it (a warm coat on a winter day); while desire is directed at the object that provoked it (in my case: a beautiful woman, a piece of music by Bach, a good book). The thing is, while a need can be satisfied, satisfying a desire is quite a rarity. Personally, I believe I'll never be able to say I've seen enough beautiful women, heard enough fine music, or read enough good books. Slovenian philosopher Slavoj Žižek remarked that the *raison d'être* of desire is not to be satisfied, but to expand – desires don't want to be closed, but always want to want more.

Being as fond of lists and tables as I am, I couldn't help myself: I prepared a table of desires. Before we go there, I'd like to remind my readers of that fundamental insight I expressed (on page 47) regarding trivial and profound truths. This is particularly appropriate when it comes to the field of desires: we may have conflicting desires, and this often applies to the strongest desires we have.

Feel free to add some of your own, if you so desire.

to love	to be loved	knowledge
to see	to hear	to speak
sexual desire	food	happiness
fame	meaning	money
power	eternal life	authenticity
appreciation	boredom	ignorance
the desire to forego desires		

Ten Little Remarks about Big Desires

Remark 1

Clearly, Love is desire. We all desire more love. We'll never say we loved or were loved enough.

In *The Banquet*, Plato (with Phaedrus as his mouthpiece) argued that in every couple, one loves more and the other is loved more. Most of us desire both: to love and to be loved. French writer George Sand said that the greatest happiness possible is to love and be loved in return (her words were slightly modified by Eden Ahbez for Nat King Cole's song 'Nature Boy').

But things don't always work out the way we want them to. Polish painter and journalist Janina Ipohorska once wrote: 'I love and am loved; I'm only sorry it is not the same man.'

Remark 2

Some of you may be surprised to see that I included Boredom in the list of desires, but boredom is our desire to have a desire. I'd love to think that I came up with this idea, but I'm not so sure – I may have read something like it in Tolstoy's works.

Remark 3

Do we desire Knowledge? Do we really want to know? Well, some things we do and some things we don't. Lacan maintained that, contrary to the view whereby curiosity (*Wissenstrieb*) is innate, 'I don't want to know' is actually the basic and spontaneous position of human beings.

Let me give you an example. I don't believe there are many among us who want to know when they will die. Not knowing our expiration date makes us all slightly immortal. By the same token, animals are not even aware that they will die, and thus they live outside the dimension of time: theirs is the kingdom of eternity.

One of the Greek myths I find most horrid speaks of a punishment meted out to the Cyclops who was informed of the day of his death. I believe that for quite a few humans whose life is already hard, knowing when it will all end would make life intolerable.

For me, one of the most moving stories about life with a deadline appears in a scene from Ridley Scott's movie *Blade Runner* (based on a Philip K Dick story), in which replicant (android) Roy, who loves life, begs his maker to revoke his expiry date and give him some more time. Just like most of us, Roy wants more life. Though this doesn't happen, Roy spends his last moments saving the man who was sent to kill him. Roy doesn't only love his own life: he loves Life.

I know I've chosen quite an extreme example, but there are many other things, except the time of our death, that we would not like to know, including things that happened, things that are about to happen, things about ourselves, and things about others whom we love or hate.

Emmanuel Kant was bothered by the question 'What can be known?' and Friedrich Nietzsche asked, 'What is worth knowing?' The wise medieval Jewish physician and thinker Maimonides had an interesting view of the Tree of Knowledge in the Book of Genesis, believing that Adam and Eve *did the right thing* when they ate fruit from the Tree, even though they risked the death penalty by doing so. Maimonides felt that living as an aware and knowing human being is better than being stuck forever in a Fool's Paradise, having no mind or wisdom. According to him, curiosity is not a sin, and the omniscient God who created us in His image knew that we would forever seek knowledge.

Aware of these two conflicting desires, Socrates believed that the desire for knowledge is the utmost good, while the desire to be ignorant is absolute evil. He felt that a life unquestioned is not worth living, and demanded: 'Know thyself!'

Others, however, thought that knowing yourself is a blessing in disguise, at best. Johann Wolfgang von Goethe, for example, disagreed with Socrates: 'If I knew myself, I'd try to run away; but how can I run from myself, and where would I go when I carry myself with me always?'

Polish sci-fi writer Stanisław Lem took man's encounter with 'himself' a step further. In *Solaris*, he describes how people who face things hidden deep inside their minds actually go mad and even commit suicide. Sometimes, ignorance is bliss.

Personally, I have no problem with both views on knowledge, because we've all realized at some point or other that profound truths are usually countered by other profound truths. As humans, we have a desire to know, but also a desire to be ignorant, and the two are not mutually exclusive.

On the one hand, 'Then I saw that wisdom excelleth folly, as far as light excelleth darkness' (Ecclesiastes 2:13), while on the other, 'For in much wisdom is much grief, and he that increaseth knowledge increaseth sorrow' (Ecclesiastes 1:18).

The 1,000 Masks Experiment (inspired by Nietzsche)

If you set out to closely know thyself, and if you think you have the courage to do so by removing all the masks you are wearing, try the following experiment. Choose a quiet room. Go in. Turn off the lights, close all windows and curtains, eliminate all possible sources of noise or any other form of disturbance, and sit quietly. Rest a while, focus, and ask yourself the following questions: Who am I *really*? What do I *really* want to do with myself? What would I do if anything were possible? Who do I love? Who do I hate? Why do I hate them? Do I envy others? Who are they? Why do I envy them? Ignoring all social conventions, how do I truly feel about my parents, partner and siblings? What was my worst thought ever? Can I be trusted at the moment of truth? Am I courageous? Do I fear death? Am I being honest with myself right now as I answer these questions?

Nietzsche remarked that it's no accident that the source of the English word 'person' is the Latin term *persona* – namely, 'mask' or 'role'. I find this etymology profound. Indeed, we're all wearing masks and playing roles all the time. We are pretenders.

On that note, I strongly recommend that you take the time and, the first chance you get, catch Ingmar Bergman's insightful film *Persona*. One of the movie's characters completely stops talking, realizing that everything she says is a lie.

We are so used to pretending in the presence of others, that we fail to notice that we pretend even when we are alone.

When we try to fool others, it sometimes works and sometimes doesn't. But when we attempt to fool ourselves, our success rates are phenomenal, with one success following another.

One of the most interesting things about the mask experiment is the fact that once we remove a mask, we're surprised to find another mask right underneath it. That mask is harder to remove, but if we succeed ... we discover another mask. It seems endless. We have multiple layers of masks that prevent us from truly getting to know ourselves (I suspect this is for mental health reasons).

The farthest I've ever got to was my third mask. After that, it became too scary. People who are not scared by this experiment are either doing it wrong or living in endless denial.

Remark 4

Sexual desire looms large. Well, you know what I mean. Henry Miller once said: 'Sex is one of the nine reasons for reincarnation ... The other eight are unimportant.' Enough said.

Remark 5

There's often a strong desire for things that are Real. The 20th and 21st centuries are filled with forgery and falsehood. Here's a partial list: we have decaffeinated coffee; alcohol-free beer; soft drinks with fewer calories and less taste (how did they ever manage to convince us they were even drinkable?); sugar- and cholesterol-free cakes; virtual sex; books without words; wars fought with no enemy in sight; reality shows instead of real life; bourgeois weekend spirituality instead of real inner work; people without personalities; meaningless words; Facebook 'friends' instead of real friendships; polite idioms instead of manners or caring; never-ending soap operas that replace our real lives; couch sports; people who spend their time and money on changing their appearance; trivial pursuits instead of seeking knowledge and understanding – and I'm only warming up here, so don't get me started!

Is there anything real left? I believe that pain is always real, and true love must be. It's no wonder that young people turn up blind alleys seeking the Real.

To be absolutely true and honest is to live with your heart on your sleeve. It means losing control. Most people are so scared that others might know what they really think and fear, who they truly love and who they hate – that they keep everything bottled up inside. This is why Nietzsche believed that lying is fundamental for human existence, and why Chekhov said that most people's real lives take place inside the secret compartments of their hearts that only they can access.

Remark 6

The desire to be happy is shared by all humans. There are countless variations of happiness and the word itself could mean whatever you want it to mean – but it's a basic human desire. However, it might be a double-edged sword.

Einstein remarked that he would rather solve complicated equations than be happy, but I believe – with all due respect – that he too wanted to be happy and that solving equations was his way to get there.

Certain psychologists maintain that 'happiness is the betrayal of desires', while others argue that 'desire betrays happiness'; and some psychoanalysts view the denial of all desires as bliss.

In Buddhist tradition, *tanha* (desire or thirst) is the source of almost all human trouble, strife and suffering. When you entertain a passion for happiness, the Buddha said, you're actually betraying your happiness, because you cannot be happy when you desire to be happy.

A word of caution, though, before we decide to renounce our desires: even Buddhist monks might succumb to the desire to forsake all desires.

Desire in the mind is the real impurity and a very great evil.

Swami Sivananda

I do not totally agree with the psychoanalysts or with the Buddhist monks. I guess it all depends on where you want to go. As for me, I have certain desires that I greatly enjoy, and I would love to be their slave (though I'd gladly renounce others).

Remark 7

The desires to See, Hear and Speak are deep-rooted. Just observe people around you and see how these three-in-one desires play out. We could travel the world far and wide, and still not be satisfied with the vistas we saw. A friend once asked me why I travelled to Switzerland (apparently, he felt it was a boring country). If I died without ever seeing Switzerland, I replied, and went to the Afterlife for a discussion of my next abode, I'd run the risk of upsetting God. After all, He worked hard to create the Jungfrau and the Creux du Van and the Trümmelbach Falls, so the least I can do is make the effort to see them.

The book you're reading now was born out my desire to talk about things that interest me. I hope that you too, my dear reader, view this book as a conversation between friends. Yes, I can hear you.

I write because I cannot help it. I write comments in the margins of books I read. I have notebooks in which I write down ideas when they come to mind or songs that I enjoyed. I type words and sentences on my keyboard and place them in my hard drive. I wrote even when I didn't believe that my writings would ever turn into real books, get published and find readers.

Remark 8

Diotima, a wise Greek woman, was the one who told Socrates that we only desire that which we 'do not own'. She further educated him that the harder it is to gain something, the more we desire it. Gaining immortality is absolutely impossible, which is why it has always been one of the greatest human desires. Yet, speaking of ancient Greeks, let me remind you that when Odysseus was offered immortality (the nymph Calypso desired to make him her immortal husband), he declined and said, 'I want to go home.' Yes, things are *always* more complicated than they seem.

Remark 9

Most of us strongly desire a Meaningful Life. We don't want to remain as actors on the stage of life after the director has stopped giving instructions or quit the production altogether. We need to know what role we'll play, and many of us want more lines.

> Life has to be given a meaning because of the obvious fact that it has no meaning.
>
> Henry Miller

Remark 10

The desire for Appreciation is formidable. I once heard that shortly after William James completed *The Principles of Psychology*, his monumental, 1,200-page double volume, he said it should be destroyed, because in the process of writing it he failed to consider the deepest human desire: the desire for appreciation.

Naturally, all of us want to feel appreciated. We want our parents, friends and even enemies to think kindly if not highly of us. We even want the appreciation of people we don't care about at all ('What will the neighbours say?') – or even complete strangers.

> Deep down in his private heart no man much respects himself.

Mark Twain

We all want to be envied. We want to be famous. Dostoevsky and Nietzsche, as I've mentioned above, shared the insight that people who despise themselves esteem themselves as self-despisers. Rabindranath Tagore remarked that even very wise and old people try to make a good impression, and that we all enjoy compliments even if we know they aren't genuine. Furthermore, people who tend to reject our compliments are actually fishing for more and asking us to repeat them.

In all of us there is, to some degree, a little of the conceited man who meets the Little Prince. Still, as we've found out by now, nothing is simple. Delusions of grandeur and an inferiority complex often cohabit in the psyche of the same person.

French mathematician and philosopher Blaise Pascal used to wear a belt with sharp metal spikes on the inner side. Whenever he noticed he was bragging and trying to impress others, or even just himself, he would pull hard on that belt. I find this attitude a bit too severe. For me, the desire to win people's appreciation is human, provided it's proportionate. And even if it's wrong, there are much worse things in our psychological make-up to worry about.

The Desire to Rule and to Judge (the Prince meets a king)

In the first asteroid he visits on his voyage, the Little Prince meets an old and strange king who has an uncontrollable urge to dominate the world and command everyone. But he is also a wise leader and issues only sensible orders (which is quite rare, I must add). Tired from his long journey, the prince yawns while facing the king.

'It is contrary to etiquette to yawn in the presence of a king,' the monarch said to him. 'I forbid you to do so.'

'I can't help it. I can't stop myself,' replied the Little Prince, thoroughly embarrassed. 'I have come on a long journey, and I have had no sleep …'

'Ah, then,' the king said. 'I order you to yawn. It is years since I have seen anyone yawning. Yawns, to me, are objects of curiosity. Come, now! Yawn again! It is an order.'

You see how moderate and reasonable that king is being? He soon adds:

'If I ordered a general … to change himself into a seabird, and if the general did not obey me, that would not be the fault of the general. It would be my fault.'

Not all rulers are like that king. Many leaders order their subordinates to do really absurd things, and often they are heeded. History is full of such examples, mostly tragic ones.

Nothing appears more surprising to those who consider human affairs with a philosophical eye than the easiness with which the many are governed by the few.

David Hume

The king, who very much wants such a charming subject, decides to tempt the Prince to stay and even offers to make him a minister, and not just any minister, but Minister of Justice. When the Little Prince remarks that 'there is nobody here to judge', the king says:

'Then you shall judge yourself. That is the most difficult thing of all. It is much more difficult to judge oneself than to judge others. If you succeed in judging yourself rightly, then you are indeed a man of true wisdom.'

In Chapter 1 on Happiness, we already discussed the question of why people so easily believe everything bad they hear about others, but doubt the good things they hear about them. Remember La Rochefoucauld's reply? 'If we had no *faults* of our own, we would not take so much pleasure in noticing those of others.'

It appears that our desire to judge others may spring from guilt. Yet Dostoevsky believed that our impulse to judge and to punish is linked with the strong urge for vengeance that people have. After the French Revolution, the infamous Marquis de Sade was made a judge, but was fired soon after because he failed to employ the guillotine enough. The marquis, whose name is the origin of the word 'sadism', was found to be not cruel enough! He felt that when occupying the judge's bench you should not harm people. It seemed perfectly logical for him to kill a man in a fit of rage, but separating a person from his head in cold blood – that was too much even for him.

A Chinese saying recommends that we judge no one before we walk a thousand miles in their shoes. The New Testament calls on us to look at the whole picture: 'And why beholdest thou the mote that is in thy brother's eye, but considerest not the beam that is in thine own eye? Or how wilt thou say to thy brother, Let me pull out the mote out of thine eye; and, behold, a beam is in thine own eye? Thou hypocrite, first cast out the beam out of thine own eye; and then shalt thou see clearly to cast out the mote out of thy brother's eye' (Matthew 7:3–5). And Jewish sage Hillel suggested: '*Judge* not thy friend until thou standest in his place' (*Ethics of the Fathers*).

Be kind, for everyone you meet is fighting a hard battle.

Plato

The way I read Hillel's remarks is: '*Never* judge thy friend', because you'll never stand in exactly the same place as him. And if, by some miracle, I do find myself standing in his place, then I'm exactly like him, and there's no justification for me to judge him.

How can anyone judge another? Who can tell whose blood is redder? The beggar in the street corner may be dearer to God than the scholar or the VIP. The beggar could have done deeds that God holds dearer than anything a monarch has done.

Certain people treat others as if they were invisible, particularly when they consider themselves to be important. Is the guard at the university gate less important than the professors he welcomes every day? To whom? Why?

Before God, we are all equally wise – and equally foolish.

Albert Einstein

I was lucky enough to attend a lecture by the Dalai Lama when he spoke of the connection between our tendency to judge others, our anger and our wisdom. He remarked that anger always contains a misplaced desire to judge. For example, when we stand at a traffic light and someone behind us honks the minute the light turns green, our hearts are filled with anger and we judge that person severely. If we do that, we're making a mistake, the Dalai Lama said. Who knows why that person honked? Perhaps he's rushing to the hospital. It could be a soccer mom, late, speeding to pick up her stranded daughter. Perhaps it's a man who was just told he was seriously ill and is now a nervous wreck. The truth is that we know nothing about the source of that honk, and so a wise person shouldn't get angry or judge.

When the Little Prince eventually decides to go back on the road and judge himself elsewhere, the king can't just let him go.

'I make you my Ambassador,' the king called out, hastily.
He had a magnificent air of authority.
'The grown-ups are very strange,' the Little Prince said to himself, as he continued on his journey.

Antoine de Saint-Exupéry, *The Little Prince*

How Much Is Enough?

So what's the story with money? Well, some people understand that they need money and so it's quite possible that they will satisfy that need at some point. If, however, they start desiring money, no amount of gold will quench their thirst.

Antoine de Saint-Exupéry shed plenty of light on the issue. In the fourth planet that the Little Prince visits, he finds a businessman who is busy counting stars, believing they belong to him, and hoping to purchase more and more stars by selling those he owns.

When the Prince inquires about the benefit the businessman derives from 'owning' so many stars, he answers:

'I write the number of my stars on a little paper. And then I put this paper in a drawer and lock it with a key.'

The entire chapter is a deep parody about money. After all, a $100 bill by itself is worth nothing at all. It's worth whatever we decide ... or rather, whatever we decide to pretend it's worth.

Furthermore, why should we care about what our bank balance says? If that balance reads 100 million, does this make us happier than, say, 88 million? Most of us do have such a total written or printed on a sheet of paper (or computer software) and locked away in some drawer or file, and the larger that number, the more content and satisfied we are, just like that businessman.

This is all very strange indeed. Looks like we have no choice but to ask Baruch Spinoza for some input. After he explained vanity so nicely, I wonder how he feels about greed.

Well, he has plenty to say, so let me summarize his view: greed, he believes, is an unrestrained passion and uncontrollable desire for an excess of assets.

How Much Land Does a Man Need? (based very freely on a Tolstoy story)

Boris Landovsky had a strange hobby. He loved to collect land. He already had plenty of territory, but remember: a desire cannot be satisfied. Boris even used to joke about his passion: 'I don't need all the land in the world. I just want the plots that border on mine,' he would tell his friends. And he would smile, pleased with himself.

One day he rose earlier than usual and set out to find a place where he could buy plenty of land for the lowest price possible. Yet, even though he started out early and was in the mood for shopping, it was not a good day. The land he found was either not good enough, or too expensive, or not for sale. At noon, having bought nothing, he decided to go for a drink in a village pub.

As he sat there, gloomy and sad, three bearded Chechens approached him. They wanted to sell their plot and heard he was buying. 'We have a lot of land, and the soil is good too, and our price is quite low,' the bearded Chechens said.

'Where is your land?' Boris asked, and a spark of excitement appeared in his eye.

'A 15-minute walk from here,' the Chechens estimated.

'Shall we?' Boris suggested.

After a 15-minute walk, the three Chechens and Mr Landovsky arrived at a magnificent field, spreading green and wide as far as the eye could see.

'What do you want for this land?' the merchant inquired.

'Well, the deal is quite simple,' the Chechens said. 'You give us 100 roubles, and then you have till sunset to choose the size of the plot you want. You do that by simply walking around it. Whatever land you encircle by foot … is yours. There is, however, just one very strict rule: you must make a full circle while the sun is in the sky. If you fail to return to your starting point by sunset, you lose your money.'

'You can't be serious?' Boris said, sceptically.

'Chechens are always serious,' they said very seriously.

'So why am I wasting time? Here's your 100 roubles. May I start walking now?'

'Go right ahead,' they said.

Mr Landovsky set off. 'I've never made such a wonderful deal,' he thought. 'I'd better make the best of it.' After walking for a minute or two, he started running. This was a rare opportunity, since all he had to do was make a circle around the plot he desired in order to make the most of it. The serious, bearded Chechens watched him as he ran farther and farther away from them, and Mr Landovsky looked up to make sure the sun was in the right place. It was well above him.

He kept running. He ran and ran, and there was only one thought in his head: 'I must run just a little more, I must not waste a piece of land here. I'm sure I'll make it to the starting point on time. What would be a good time to start running back? Not now. Not yet. I need more land.'

Mr Landovsky glanced at the sun again and was surprised to see it was not that high any more. He decided it was time to go back (though he was not pleased with this decision) and started running faster to beat the deadline. To his amazement, two sad facts became immediately apparent to him. First, it is rather difficult to run fast after you have been running for several hours, particularly if you are over 40. Second, when you are in a hurry to beat the sunset, the sun starts descending twice as fast as it does on ordinary days.

Our Boris (let us drop the formality) ran as fast as he could, but the pain in his left side was growing intolerable, blood pumped hard in his veins and his lungs could not get enough air.

Seeing the Chechens standing on the horizon, he gave it a final push. The sun disappeared from view, leaving a red glimmer on the horizon. He reached the starting point.

'It's mine! The land is all mine!' he thought in a daze.

Sadly, that was his last thought. Boris collapsed and passed away.

'Well, the amount of land a man truly needs is two by six feet under,' the Chechens seriously said to each other as they covered the fresh grave with rich soil.

Incidentally, Tolstoy loved purchasing land when he was young. It's quite possible that he dedicated that story to himself. (The great Irish novelist James Joyce wrote to his daughter that 'How Much Land Does a Man Need?' is 'the greatest story that the literature of the world knows'.) It appears that Tolstoy the writer was much wiser than Tolstoy the man.

So, we've learned that greed is not a good thing. So what? Why, then, do so many people admire figures – from Tutankhamun to the modern world's oligarchs – who were acquisitive and had almost everything they coveted? These days no one is really ashamed of their wealth.

It's no shame to be poor … but it's no great honour either.

Tevye the Dairyman, in *Fiddler on the Roof*

In fact, Tolstoy believed that a good man cannot be rich and a rich man cannot be good. Late in his life, he actually loathed property and riches.

However, we must not rush to conclusions.

In the USSR tens of millions of people were murdered by two sworn money-haters, Lenin and Stalin. Extremism is never a good idea.

All empty souls tend toward extreme opinions.

William Butler Yeats

Nevertheless, while it's wrong to hate money, we shouldn't crave it too much either. Aristotle said that the right approach to almost anything is somewhere in between the extremes, though usually not quite at the very middle.

Greed is a desire that can't be satisfied, because people not only want to be rich, they want to be richer. That is, richer than everybody else – and that's a real problem.

The following dialogue is taken from the movie *Wall Street: Money Never Sleeps*. Jacob is a young and ambitious trader who tries to pick the brain of Bretton, the head of an investment bank and the film's villain.

Jacob: What's your number?
Bretton: Excuse me?
Jacob: The amount of money you would need to be able to walk away from it all and just live happily ever after. See, I find that everyone has a number and it's usually an exact number, so what's yours?
Bretton: More.

For what is a man profited, if he shall gain the whole world, and lose his own soul? Or what shall a man give in exchange for his soul?

Matthew 16:27

Benjamin Franklin argued that money never made a single person happy. Furthermore, as one of the founding fathers of the land of the free and the brave, Franklin believed that it's in the nature of money to prevent all chances of happiness. The great American maintained that money activates a mental apparatus in people that makes them desire money in direct proportion to the amount of money they already own. That is, the more money a person has, the more bills and coins they feel they need. At a certain point, many of those money-grabbers even forget what money is for, and simply keep collecting more of it.

A money lover will never be satisfied, because passions are hard to gratify.

I resent hypocrisy, however, which is why I cannot say that money is not important. It is. I am, therefore, always surprised when I come across some weird academic study that refutes the correlation between happiness and wealth. Clearly, the authors of those studies have never really starved, nor was money ever missing from their pockets. Of course happiness and wealth are connected! It's much nicer to write a book while sitting in a splendid room in a large house overlooking an enchanted lake than to do the same in a single-bedroom apartment in a poor and violent neighbourhood. Disdaining money is much nicer when one sits at the top of society's heap of power and glory than feeling the same way on the margins of society. I do not dismiss money. All I'm saying is that we should heed Schopenhauer and not believe that money is all we need, and we should avoid turning money into a passion that overrides every other passion we have.

> At the door of the miserable rich man sleeps the contented beggar.
>
> Tibetan saying

Geography Lesson

On the sixth planet, the Little Prince meets a geographer who spends his days drawing maps, but never leaves his desk. As the conversation between the two unfolds, the prince begins to question the geographer's desire, the impulse that motivates 'the old gentleman who wrote voluminous books'. Was it the desire to gain knowledge or the desire for appreciation?

'The geographer is much too important to go loafing about. He does not leave his desk, but he receives the explorers in his study.'

(Notice how the geographer speaks of himself in the third person.)

Jean-Jacques Rousseau once remarked that no philosopher would be interested in anything if it didn't provide him with an opportunity to impress others. What can we learn about this French moralist from that remark?

I've met quite a few academics who cared about prestige much more than they concerned themselves with their field of study. They wrote the same article repeatedly, slightly modifying it to create new versions, and sent their work to scientific journals, seeking fame and wishing to feel important. Of course, most scientists aren't like that, and are nothing like the geographer either. Most of them are driven by a real desire to gain knowledge.

Let us go back, then, to our old and tedious geographer. Look at what he busies himself with! What a waste of life! Like Rabbit from the Hundred Acre Wood, the geographer knows so much that he understands nothing at all. When the Little Prince tells him that there are three volcanoes, a baobab tree and a rose on his planet, the geographer says that he doesn't care about such things.

'We do not record flowers,' said the geographer.
'Why is that? The flower is the most beautiful thing on my planet!'
'We do not record them,' said the geographer, 'because they are ephemeral.'
'What does that mean — "ephemeral"?'
'It means, that which is in danger of speedy disappearance.'

Antoine de Saint-Exupéry, *The Little Prince*

All beauty must die.

Traditional wisdom, expressed by Nick Cave and others

Here now is a short postscript on desire. I once heard a lecture by an educated person who attempted to teach us, his listeners, how to manage desires instead of letting them manage us. The lecture was perfectly delivered, but still, I could not relate to it. I don't believe we can eliminate our desires, or even guide them in certain directions. I share Baruch Spinoza's view that the only way to overcome a desire is by having a stronger desire. That philosophical luminary advised that we try to connect with the greatest desire of all – loving God (if you can cultivate a certain mental flexibility, you could interpret this 'loving God' approach by the 'philosopher of philosophers' as endless love for the world we live in). According to wise Baruch, loving God shall bestow the greatest joy upon us; but he also reminded us that the most beautiful things are necessarily rare.

3.

Imagination

We are all born originals –
why is it so many of us die copies?

Edward Young, *Night Thoughts*

One of very many Internet sites devoted to *The Little Prince* opens with a drawing of a hat, after which we're asked whether the drawing frightens us. If we answer 'no', we are denied access to the site. Stating we are not afraid of that drawing indicates that we are members of the unimaginative adult tribe, to whom everything must be explained.

Children and imaginative grownups (or people who read and understood *The Little Prince* and took it into their hearts) know that, of course, this is not a hat, but a snake, a boa constrictor digesting an elephant, and should be feared.

How could we have missed that before?

One of the world's greatest minds said it very simply:

Imagination is more important than knowledge.

Albert Einstein

'See Me and Lewis Down by the Schoolyard'

As you may recall, Lewis Carroll, author of *Alice in Wonderland*, knew that children are much wiser than adults, and that the root of the problem is school. It was no accident that he viewed the word 'lesson' as originating from 'less', meaning: the more facts we learn at school, the less we are able to marvel at the world and be amazed by things.

Lessons lessen our ability to be who we really are, to understand things, and to have dreams. They almost totally eliminate the number of interesting questions we can ask.

R D Laing sarcastically remarked: 'Children do not give up their innate imagination, curiosity, dreaminess easily. You have to love them to get them to do that.'

Antoine de Saint-Exupéry thought that the powers of imagination weaken with age, as does the distinction between things that matter and all other things. One of the reasons I became a mathematician in my 20s and engaged in mathematics for many years was the fact that I seldom attended ordinary school classes. Since I was a member of the Pythagoras Circle – a special class for curious children – I was relieved of the duty to attend normal classes, and I discovered the beauty and charm of mathematics without being bored to death by studying the usual lessons.

You really have to have a particular kind of brain to be fascinated by questions that involve three taps that (for some obscure reason) try to fill a pool while two other taps are trying to empty it. Can anyone be truly interested in figuring out how long it will take for this totally senseless procedure to end? Exposure to such questions for years (not to mention months of working on quadratic equations) is absolutely destructive. Not many know this, but true maths has nothing to do with calculating. True maths deals with beauty and thinking.

Mathematics is the music of reason.

James Joseph Sylvester (British mathematician)

The great French writer Marcel Proust believed that artists and children look at the world the right way. He did not mean to say that we should all be painters, poets, or childish, but that we should notice and pay attention to clouds and flowers, the wind on our faces, the taste of a petite madeleine, the smell of fresh bread, the sound of raindrops. Children can do that enviably. They can spend minutes just jumping and splashing around in street puddles, or admire the sound of clinking pot covers.

Furthermore, I honestly believe (OK, I know) that certain childlike qualities – such as wonderment and unbounded imagination – can not only be preserved in conscious adulthood, but they can even be developed further and taken to much higher levels.

A leaf of grass is no less than the journey-work of the stars.

Walt Whitman, 'Song of Myself'

A fool sees not the same tree that a wise man sees.

William Blake, 'Proverbs of Hell'

There's a lovely scene in *American Beauty*, a film by Sam Mendes, where the protagonist finds incredible beauty in everything, including an empty plastic bag twirling in the breeze. It reminds me of William Blake:

To see a World in a Grain of Sand
And a Heaven in a Wild Flower,
Hold Infinity in the palm of your hand
And Eternity in an hour.

William Blake, 'Auguries of Innocence'

Fly Me to the Moon

What happens to us adults? Have we completely lost the ability to marvel, admire and find beauty in everything?

It seems to me that many members of the adult clan have indeed lost these abilities.

Once I watched a candid camera show on a European TV channel. It showed people in an airport, as the PA system announced: 'Flights to the moon are leaving at gate nine. All passengers, please report to the gate.' Did anyone in the terminal faint with amazement? Not one. A woman they interviewed there said it was the first time she'd heard about flights to the moon, but she always knew it would happen one day.

Speaking of flights to the moon, let us not forget the planets and stars. Isn't a starry night an amazing sight? I guess the only reason people aren't amazed by it is the fact that this miracle happens much too often – every night, in fact, in some regions.

R W Emerson's words, 'If the stars should appear one night in a thousand years, how would men believe and adore, and preserve for many generations the remembrance of the City of God which had been shown!', inspired the great sci-fi author Isaac Asimov to write his famous 1941 novel Nightfall. Now, try to imagine that sight of the starry heavens appearing before our eyes once in a decade. How eagerly we would await it! We would all stand there, looking upward in admiration and awe.

Freud Attempts to Cross the Ocean

In *Civilization and Its Discontents* (1930) Sigmund Freud related that a friend of his experienced what he called an 'oceanic feeling'. Freud was speaking about Romain Rolland, who in 1927 wrote to him and described that feeling after reading Freud's *The Future of an Illusion*, which had been published in the same year and discusses the origins of religion, which Freud views as merely an illusion.

'Oceanic feeling' was the term Rolland used to describe that sense of awe at everything that fills our hearts and minds when we realize that there exists something eternal, or at least boundless like the ocean. A moment of grace when everything is as it should be. An oceanic feeling is a combination of wonderment and endless gratitude. Freud admitted he never felt that.

The Art of Wonderment (on lesser and greater miracles)

When the circus show started, no one could have expected how it would end. The juggler took five balls out of his bag and then threw them up in the air, making them chase each other in perfect order and return to his skilled hands. He then tossed them up again, and then added another and another. More and more balls joined the show, but the crowd did not seem very impressed. Then, after a few minutes of tedious juggling with ten balls, something happened that no one had ever seen before.

The onlookers watched in amazement as balls flew up and just hung in the air, refusing to fall. Ten balls reached the top of the circus tent and floated there, motionless. The crowd gasped. Then the juggler removed ten more balls from his bag, threw them up in the air and made them spin around the first ten stationary balls. Then he threw up ten more, and then another ten. The crowd watched in amazement as dozens of balls performed an unbelievable stunt: some of them were just hanging there, while others circled around them, and still others just moved around chaotically.

Then the crowd noticed, not knowing how it had happened, that the juggler had vanished, leaving behind an amazing spectacle.

'This is amazing! I've never seen anything like it. It's a real miracle,' members of the crowd yelled.

If you think this is a miracle, what do you think about the amazing spectacle of celestial bodies out in space?

I have an oceanic feeling when I make love to the lady I love; when I listen to the Adagio from Ravel's Piano Concerto in G minor performed by Arturo Benedetti Michelangeli, or to Allegri's *Miserere*; when I walk along the beach in the winter and then have a cup of coffee in a beachfront café; when I read Chekhov's story 'The Lady with the Dog' for the umpteenth time; when I look at Giorgione's *Sleeping Venus* or at Titian's *Venus of Urbino*, or watch Isabelle Adjani bathing in a tub in the movie *One Deadly Summer*; when I read S Y Agnon's *Simple Story*, or *Psychological Topology of the Way* by Georgian philosopher Merab Mamardashvili; when I listen to Astor Piazzolla playing the tango *Oblivion*; when I visit the Italian Dolomites or picturesque Urbino, or when I tour Jerusalem, which traditionally took nine of the world's ten measures of beauty; and every time I hug my daughters.

A Prayer

Teach me, my Lord, to count my blessings and pray

For the secret in a withering leaf, for glowing ripeness in
a pear,
The freedom to see, to feel and breathe more,
To know, to aspire and to stray.
Teach my lips blessings and songs of praise
As your time renews morning and night, always
So that my day today is not as it was before,
So that my days are never habitual.

Lea Goldberg

Romain Rolland (who, I am certain, would have loved that Goldberg poem if he had known it) remarked that an 'oceanic feeling' is a type of religious sensation that's far removed from any customary religious dogma, ceremony or afterlife concerns. I honestly believe that our ability to experience oceanic feelings is a prerequisite of our ability to experience true moments of joy.

Freud noted that Rolland's letter astonished and disturbed him for quite some time. In fact, he answered it only two years later. Freud was amazed that an educated person such as Rolland was capable of even experiencing such primitive feelings (as Freud characterized them).

It can't be helped. Even great minds such as Freud's have a hard time releasing the 'false consensus effect' and ceasing to think that everybody thinks the way they themselves do. And he wasn't alone. Our beloved Pooh too believed that if he loved honey, then heffalumps must love it too.

We are all very different from one another, and each individual has a world of his own. I know people who don't like Mozart's music, people who couldn't care less about money, people who never eat strawberries, people who donate a kidney to total strangers, people who are afraid of chickens. I even know a few people who are not a bit interested in Goldbach's Conjecture or in Fermat's Last Theorem, though I, being a mathematician, find this odd.

The fact is, the Little Prince erred, believing that the boundaries of his imagination reflected the absolute truth. He was very quick to judge others and believed that the echo he heard was the sound of people repeating his words.

The people have no imagination. They repeat whatever one says to them … On my planet I had a flower; she always was the first to speak …

In another example, the view expressed by the flower he found in the desert is very far from the truth. The flower can only think about things she can see from her angle, which is a very wilderness-minded point of view. Speaking of people, she says:

'I think there are six or seven of them in existence. I saw them, several years ago. But one never knows where to find them. The wind blows them away. They have no roots, and that makes their life very difficult.'

Are we not all a little like that flower that lives in the desert?

The world is indeed stranger than anything our rational mind can grasp.

Albert Einstein

The African Who Dreamed up Snow

One of the criteria for identifying genius should perhaps be the ability to accept that the boundaries of our imagination are not the boundaries of the world. That ability is what motivates people to push known boundaries and expand their minds.

The Tale of the Man and the Newspaper (inspired by John Allen Paulos and Ludwig Wittgenstein)

On a particularly hot summer day, a man who was walking down the street stopped at a kiosk to buy a cold drink. As he drank, his gaze fell upon a newspaper headline that he found most amazing. The man could not believe his eyes. Realizing that this was merely a newspaper headline, he decided to investigate the issue further. He asked for another copy of the newspaper, and there it was – the unbelievable headline again, right on the front page. Amazed at the words he read, the man decided to buy all 36 copies of the newspaper that were on sale at that particular kiosk. The man took the newspapers home, where he sat down and checked each and every copy. When he realized that the same story appeared in every one of them, he became convinced it was the truth.

Most of us, hearing this Wittgensteinesque story for the first time, would immediately think: 'How silly can you be?! No one in their sound mind would read 36 copies of the same newspaper to be convinced that a story is true.' Wittgenstein believed that, in truth, almost all humans live exactly like that. We keep reading, hearing and watching the same things, over and over again. We may think they are different, but they aren't.

Geniuses such as Einstein, Darwin or Freud wrote their own 'newspapers', and though some of their insights may have been wrong, they were more interesting and influential than correct remarks made by mediocre people. Furthermore, they even invented their own languages for those papers. These geniuses spoke in original languages because they were expressing things that had occurred to no one before them.

Genius is *an African* who dreams up snow.

Vladimir Nabokov

I find Nabokov's definition of genius both appealing and precise. To some extent, it echoes Nietzsche, who said that a genius is a person who can think of (as of yet) unnamed things. The fact is, terms we all freely use today didn't exist before they were invented by geniuses: Freud coined 'conscious' and 'subconscious', 'ego' and 'id'; and Darwin came up with 'natural selection' and 'origin of species'.

They wrote their 'newspapers' in the languages they created, but once those 'newspapers' became institutionalized, everyone wrote and read more or less the same newspapers. It takes people of stature to write different and new 'newspapers' and, more often than not, these new 'newspapers' are not welcome. People with original ideas have often had to pay dearly for them.

One of the best-known cases of a person who paid for his original ideas with his life is Giordano Bruno, who was burned at the stake in the Campo dei Fiori in Rome because he dared to go public with a series of ideas that were unheard of in his day. Among other things, he claimed there was a mistake in Aristotle's 'newspaper,' and argued that the Earth is not the centre of the universe. Actually, Bruno believed, the universe has no centre at all, which is very close to modern thinking. Let us not forget that Bruno lived in the second half of the 16th century! It takes a lot of wisdom and courage to establish a new newspaper (or even to publish a slightly different passage in an existing one).

Is It a Bird? Is It a Pipe?

Belgian surrealist painter René Magritte painted a pipe and wrote right underneath it: 'Ceci n'est pas une pipe' (French for: 'This is not a pipe').

What could he possibly mean? We can all see it's a pipe, so why did Magritte write that it isn't?

If we consider this for a while, we'll soon realize that Magritte was absolutely right. What we have before us is not a pipe, of course. It is a painting of a pipe, and a pipe and a painting of a pipe are two totally different things.

In the same way, the world we see is not the 'real' world. What we 'see' is just an impression of the world, which our senses constantly paint and repaint for us.

If I had microscopic vision, for example, I could see molecules whirling in the air in my room and admire their neat arrangement.

A spoon in a glass of water does not really break, and though we feel the Earth as solid and stable, it's actually spinning at great speed. Similarly, the land and the sky do not meet, though that's what we see on the horizon. Our senses just keep misleading us.

This world is but a canvas to our imaginations.

Henry David Thoreau

The Buddha knew that we have such little knowledge of the truth because our minds are chained by our senses. He believed our view of the world resembles that of an unhatched chick.

Similarly, Socrates believed that the truth will be revealed to us after we die, when we're finally released from the tyranny of our senses.

The Turkish Astronomer and the Armani Suit

Chapter 4 of *The Little Prince* is one of my favourites. In the beginning of the chapter, we become acquainted with a Turkish astronomer who appears before the International Astronomer's Congress in 1909, and presents a wonderful lecture about the tiny star from which the Prince has arrived. He named it Asteroid B–612. The problem is that when that Turkish astronomer gives his lecture, no one listens to him. The other astronomers see a man in ridiculous clothes – shoes with points that curl backward, a shirt that connects with strange trousers to form a sort of overall, and a very funny hat on top. 'It is impossible for a man dressed like that to know anything about anything at all,' the astronomers tell each other, and they go to the cafeteria while he is still on the podium.

Antoine de Saint-Exupéry was not pleased with this kind of behaviour. He wrote:

> In the course of this life, I have had a great many encounters with a great many people who have been concerned with matters of consequence. I have lived a great deal among grown-ups. I have seen them intimately, close at hand. And that hasn't much improved my opinion of them.

That, however, was not the end of that affair:

> Fortunately, however, for the reputation of Asteroid B–612, a Turkish dictator made a law that his subjects, under pain of death, should change to European costume [preferably by Italian designers]. So in 1920 the astronomer gave his demonstration all over again, dressed with impressive style and elegance [wearing a fancy suit by Armani Sr]. And this time everybody accepted his report.

Even though he delivered the exact same lecture as he did in 1909, this time he was applauded and cheered.

Go figure the grown-ups. Only the devil knows what strange things have an impact on their power of judgement.

Drowning by Numbers (Better Homes and Gardens)

Grown-ups develop an unbridled fondness for numbers and quantifiers, and are particularly keen on asking questions that start with 'how much …?' and 'how many …?'

Several years ago, when I bought a house, I experienced exactly what Chapter 4 of *The Little Prince* describes.

The grown-ups who wanted to know things about the house posed all the wrong questions. They didn't want to know: Is it near the ocean? Does it feel like home? Do you have a terrace from which you can watch the stars? Does it have a nice garden? Is there enough room for all of your books in the basement?

> If you have a *garden* and a *library*, you have everything you need.
>
> Marcus Tullius Cicero

Instead of asking the right questions, they bugged me with queries about numbers (most of which I couldn't answer). How much did it cost? How many rooms does it have? How big was the mortgage you took for it? How many square metres of space does it contain? How much did you pay for remodelling it? How many owners did it have before you? How many stairs lead to the roof? How much this and how many that.

These days, almost everything is quantified numerically. How much do you make a month/a year? How many years did you study? What did you get in your SATs? How many times did you travel abroad last year? How much did you pay for this wine?

Grown-ups are very strange indeed.

How Wealthy Are His Parents?

Yes, grown-ups are very fond of numbers. Saint-Exupéry writes:

> When you tell them that you have made a new friend, they never ask you any questions about essential matters. They never say to you, 'What does his voice sound like? What games does he love best? Does he collect butterflies?' Instead, they demand: 'How old is he? How many brothers has he? How much does he weigh? How much money do his parents make?' Only from these figures do they think they have learned anything about him.
>
> Antoine de Saint-Exupéry, *The Little Prince*

Certain adults, however, are smarter than that. Upon hearing that Jane's daughter was seeing a young man socially, Mary wanted to know the occupation of his parents. Well, don't be misled by that. Mary may not have posed a 'how much?' question, but she was still interested in numbers. After all, we all know there is a strong and direct correlation between what people do for a living and how much they earn from it. What Mary really wanted to know was: 'How much do his parents make a year?'

> Society tells us the only thing that matters is matter – the only things that count are the things that can be counted.
>
> Laurence G Boldt, *Zen and the Art of Making a Living*

> But certainly, for us who understand life, figures are a matter of indifference!
>
> Antoine de Saint-Exupéry, *The Little Prince*

Rich Wines = Rich Owners

Once, when we were young, we could drink a glass of wine and opine: 'I like it,' or 'I don't like it.' Things are not that simple anymore. Today, before you even taste the wine, its owners let you know that it's a Vino Nobile di Montepulciano 1997, and that they paid $85 a bottle. What do I do now? Will I dare say it isn't to my taste after hearing these figures? (This was just a small example. Dear residents of Montepulciano, that enchanted Italian town, please don't be offended. It is my favourite wine.)

Would we really relish Beluga caviar from the Caspian Sea so much if it didn't cost an arm and a leg? And if the price of water started soaring, would we not immensely enjoy a glass of pure water?

I once asked a leading chef to name his favourite dish. I asked him to be honest with me and not name fancy-shmancy dishes such as 'bird's-nest on frog-legs served in truffle sauce and saffron with a touch of sugar-candy'. He thought for a moment and said: 'My number one dish is a really well-made thin and crisp Italian pizza. My number two, I hate to admit, is a fine dish of nicely seasoned and fresh French fries.'

Did you hear that? Pizza and chips! I mean, *children* love such foods. I always knew children had a more accurate idea of what's right.

Many adults don't have their own opinions. They believe in things because many others believe in them, want things because many others covet them, and praise a work of art because … well, because everybody does. Other grown-ups have opinions but are wary about expressing them because they want to stick with the consensus. Don't forget that amidst a cheering crowd, only a child dared to yell: 'The king is naked!'

Einstein remarked that most views that adults hold are nothing more than a rearrangement of their parents' and teachers' views. The fact that the majority hold a certain opinion does not make it the truth, and one just person is a moral majority. (Our tendency to so easily believe in views generally held by our society is known as the Bandwagon Effect.)

OK. Time to grow up, I guess.

Saint-Exupéry believed that a worthy adult is one who knows everything the other grown-ups know and yet can still look at the world with a child's eyes and candidly and courageously state his opinion. The worthy adult is the one who admires the fact that a heavy machine such as an aircraft can fly, who can see shapes in clouds, who asks why we don't feel that the Earth is turning (and why, by the way, does it spin?), who laughs at nonsense, and builds castles on a sandy beach. Only an adult who still has a child in his eyes can truly wonder at this amazing thing called Life.

4.

On Love, Briefly;
or, What the Fox Knows

Antoine and Consuelo de Saint-Exupéry

Antoine de Saint-Exupéry, author of *The Little Prince*, was born in 1900, which makes it very easy for us to know his age every year. I do not intend to present his entire biography here – enough has been written on that subject. Allow me to skip over plenty of unimportant stuff and go straight to 1926, the year in which he started working as a pilot and became one of the airmail pioneers. Saint-Ex, as his friends used to call him, worked the Toulouse–Dakar line, and if you'd seen his plane you'd probably have refused to join him on his flights. Just imagine a piece of junk with wings that hangs in the air in total defiance of the laws of physics. Saint-Ex was very fond of small planes that ran on Stone Age technology. As planes improved with time, Antoine used to say that their operators started resembling accountants more than pilots. He wrote about his dangerous adventures in *Night Flight*, a book published in 1931. But that wasn't the most important thing that happened that year.

In 1931 Antoine de Saint-Exupéry married Consuelo Sunchín Sandoval Zeceña, a painter from El Salvador who'd been a widow for two years when they met. It was love at first sight. Looking at her pictures, it isn't hard to see that Consuelo must have been a very charming lady, one whom men would easily have fallen head over heels for. Saint-Ex told his friends that he knew Consuelo would be his wife the moment he met her. Their love took them to Casablanca, Paris, Buenos Aires and New York. Their life together had periods of high passion and much tenderness, but also times of infidelity, separation and great pain. They could not live a day without each other, but were even less able to live together. Throughout their marriage, they broke up on several occasions, often for long periods, but always reunited, and they never stopped loving each other.

On 30 December 1935, Saint-Ex's plane crashed in the Sahara Desert. It was during a flight in which he and his navigator, André Prévot, attempted to fly from Paris to Saigon faster than any other crew before them. Though they crashed after spending nearly 20 hours in the air, the two aviators survived. They did, however, experience four days of great misery. Marooned in the desert, they suffered from such severe dehydration that they stopped sweating and started hallucinating. On the fourth day, just like in a Hollywood movie, they were rescued by a local camel rider.

The Little Prince, the small, poetic and philosophical book that Saint-Exupéry wrote during his 1943 stay on Long Island, New York, was closely associated with that event, but mostly it was the prettiest present he bestowed upon his beloved wife, who appears in the book as the flower, the rose that the prince loved and cared for so much. In fact, the book is their only offspring. Consuelo wrote an answer, *The Tale of the Rose*, in 1945 – after her husband went missing on 31 July 1944 while on a Second World War mission. Consuelo never published the book. The manuscript was discovered and published in 1979, some 20 years after she died.

Though lovers be lost love shall not;
And death shall have no dominion.

Dylan Thomas

Wind and Fire

One day, a very special flower appeared on the Little Prince's planet. Until then, all the flowers on his asteroid had been rather simple, with just a single row of petals. This flower, however, was different:

The shrub soon stopped growing, and began to get ready to produce a flower. The Little Prince, who was present at the first appearance of a huge bud, felt at once that some sort of miraculous apparition must emerge from it. But the flower was not satisfied to complete the preparations for her beauty in the shelter of her green chamber. … It was only in the full radiance of her beauty that she wished to appear. Oh, yes! She was a coquettish creature! And her mysterious adornment lasted for days and days.

Then one morning, exactly at sunrise, she suddenly showed herself.

And, after working with all this painstaking precision, she yawned and said:

'Ah! I am scarcely awake. I beg that you will excuse me. My petals are still all disarranged ...'

But the Little Prince could not restrain his admiration:

'Oh! How beautiful you are!'

'Am I not?' the flower responded, sweetly. 'And I was born at the same moment as the sun ...'

By now, we all know that this rose was Consuelo, and you've probably guessed that the simple flowers were all the other women that Saint-Ex had been with before he met the one and only. The passage above also makes clear that the rose isn't a particularly modest flower, and that the prince is in for a bumpy ride with her (as was reflected in the real story of Antoine and Consuelo). It's also clear, however, that the new flower is a kind of miracle for the Little Prince.

'The course of true love never did run smooth.'

Lysander, in *A Midsummer Night's Dream*, by William Shakespeare

As soon as she arrived in the world, the rose started bugging the prince:

'I think it is time for breakfast,' she added an instant later. 'If you would have the kindness to think of my needs ...'

And the little prince, completely abashed, went to look for a sprinkling-can of fresh water. So, he tended the flower.

So, too, she began very quickly to torment him with her vanity – which was, if the truth be known, a little difficult to deal with [...]

'At night I want you to put me under a glass globe. It is very cold where you live. In the place I came from ...'

But she interrupted herself at that point. She had come in the form of a seed. She could not have known anything of any other worlds. Embarrassed over having let herself be caught on the verge of such a naïve untruth, she coughed two or three times, in order to put the little prince in the wrong.

'The screen?'

'I was just going to look for it when you spoke to me …'

Then she forced her cough a little more so that he should suffer from remorse just the same.

So the little prince, in spite of all the good will that was inseparable from his love, had soon come to doubt her. He had taken seriously words which were without importance, and it made him very unhappy.

'I ought not to have listened to her,' he confided to me one day. 'One never ought to listen to the flowers. One should simply look at them and breathe their fragrance. Mine perfumed all my planet. But I did not know how to take pleasure in all her grace […]

'The fact is that I did not know how to understand anything! I ought to have judged by deeds and not by words. She cast her fragrance and her radiance over me. I ought never to have run away from her … I ought to have guessed all the affection that lay behind her poor little stratagems. Flowers are so inconsistent! But I was too young to know how to love her …'

A rose is a rose is a rose is a rose.

Gertrude Stein

To love someone is to know that person really well, and love them nonetheless.

Victor Hugo

A love that is based on 'because' or 'thanks to' will not last long if that love doesn't include 'despite of' too.

> All love that is dependent on a particular thing, when the thing ceases, the love ceases. All love that is not dependent on a particular thing, it will never cease.
>
> Ethics of the Fathers

One of the most fascinating questions I can think of is whether unconditional love exists.

Either way, when the rose blossomed into the Little Prince's life, he knew nearly nothing about love. He failed to realize that it was a miracle, that it was grace that gave him that flower. When he did finally understand that much later, it was too late.

Earlier in their relationship the Little Prince had left his rose and gone travelling, which is a good opportunity for me to present you with a criterion that will help you know whether a love you encounter is true love. I call it 'The Wind and Fire Criterion'.

It goes like this. When a fire is weak, a gust of wind can put it out; but if the fire is strong, a blowing wind will only fan the flames, and the stronger the wind, the bigger the fire will grow and the wider it will spread. It's the same with love and separation. If it isn't true love, a long separation will wash it away. If it is true, however, separation will merely reinforce it.

This is not my invention. Though I've been unable to discover who made it up, it's mentioned in various versions in numerous sources. The poem below is my favourite rendition of the idea:

> Distance does to love
> What wind gusts do to fire
> A small flame gets blown out,

A large one grows much higher.

Baruch Gefen

The Little Prince learned that truth first-hand. He nearly went out of his mind, missing and longing for his rose.

> If someone loves a flower, of which just one single blossom grows in all the millions and millions of stars, it is enough to make him happy just to look at the stars. He can say to himself, 'Somewhere, my flower is there ...' But if the sheep eats the flower, in one moment all his stars will be darkened ...

Alas, once the prince had come to understand all that, it was already too late.

On Love: Top Ten Quotes (actually a personal selection of 14 favourite insights)

Before you start reading my selection, please take a moment, think about it and write your own sentence beginning: 'Love is ...'

Now let us start our countdown.

10.

Don't ever think I fell for you, or fell over you. I didn't fall in love. I rose in it.

Toni Morrison

9.

I carry your heart with me (I carry it in my heart).

E E Cummings

My eighth place is shared by two poets: one who was born in the Land of the Rising Sun, while the other lived and wrote in the Land of Hope and Glory. Japanese poet Basho wrote a haiku:

8b.

O brightest moon of autumn.
All night long I've strolled around the pond,
in search of song.

This is a love song that doesn't mention the words we usually use in that context. Perhaps nothing could express love better than the picture of a man walking all night long around a pond. Perhaps, despite the countless words written and spoken about love, it cannot be put into words? Perhaps Raymond Carver was right when he wrote: 'It ought to make us feel ashamed when we talk like we know what we're talking about when we talk about love.'

This is Shakespeare's attempt to describe the indescribable:

8a.

All days are nights to see till I see thee,
And nights bright days when dreams do show thee me.

William Shakespeare, Sonnet 43

7.

I met in the street a very poor young man who was in love.
His hat was old, his coat worn, his cloak was out at the
elbows, the water passed through his shoes, and the stars
through his soul.

Victor Hugo

6.

Love is trembling happiness.

Khalil Gibran

The Lebanese poet is probably right. One cannot love without trembling. Every mother who loves and cares about her children knows that.

Romantic love trembles for other reasons: it might evaporate with time; jealousy might kill it; habit might put it to eternal sleep.

5.

Love is an irresistible desire to be irresistibly desired.

Robert Frost

And the Final Four:

4.

You know you're in love when you can't fall asleep because reality is finally better than your dreams.

Dr Seuss

And even if we do spoil ourselves and doze off every now and then, we could open our eyes and say the old cliché: 'You're the first thing I think of when I wake up, and the last thing on my mind when I fall asleep.'

Sufi poet Jalal al-Din Rumi even wrote a poem that combines love, sleep and God:

When I am with you, we stay up all night.
When you're not here, I can't go to sleep.
Praise God for those two insomnias!
And the difference between them.

The third place is shared by a company of three with quite similar insights: a French writer we met above, a Russian poet, and a wise woman who was a great actress and will be forever blonde:

3c.

The greatest happiness of life is the conviction that we are loved – loved for ourselves, or rather, loved in spite of ourselves.

Victor Hugo

3b.

To love a man is to see him as God had planned him, not as his parents shaped him.

Marina Tsvetaeva

3a.

I'm selfish, impatient and a little insecure. I make mistakes, I am out of control, and at times hard to handle. But if you can't handle me at my worst, then you sure as hell don't deserve me at my best.

Marilyn Monroe

The second place too is occupied jointly, by a great sci-fi novelist and a famous actress – a very pretty woman who offers a deep correction of the novelist's profound insight. We'll let the sci-fi novelist go first:

2b.

Love is that condition in which the happiness of another person is essential to your own.

Robert A Heinlein

And now the new and improved version is:

2a.

You know it's love when all you want is for that person to be happy, even if you're not part of their happiness.

Julia Roberts

Clearly, Ms Roberts is absolutely right, but the requirement she presents here seems to be much too difficult for mere mortals such as ourselves.

And now, my all-time favourite quote from my favourite writer, Count Leo Tolstoy. It appears in Chapter 14 of Part V of *Anna Karenina* – a novel that, according to Oswald Spengler, is not only the best ever written, but also the best that can *ever* be written.

Opening that chapter, Tolstoy relates:

> Levin [the similarity to Lev, Russian for Leo, is by no means accidental] had been married three months. He was happy, but not at all in the way he had expected to be. At every step he found his former dreams disappointed, and new, unexpected surprises of happiness.

One day, Levin is half an hour late coming home because he made an unsuccessful attempt to take a short and unfamiliar way, and got lost.

> He drove home thinking of nothing but her, of her love, of his own happiness, and the nearer he drew to home, the warmer was his tenderness for her.

His wife Kitty gives him a cold welcome, which quickly turns into a jealousy scene. Yet it's after that first fight the couple find themselves engaged in that Levin realizes something profound:

1.

> He felt now that he was not simply closer to her, but that he did not know where he ended and she began.

This is my best ever love quote. It would not lose its beauty or depth even if it were printed on a cheesy Valentine's Day card.

The Prince in a Garden of Roses

Travelling around the universe, the Little Prince reaches Planet Earth. The most traumatic experience he has on our planet is finding a rose garden. His rose had told him she was the only one of her kind in the entire universe. She said she was unique, that she was born with the sun, and that her petals were the most beautiful. Suddenly, the Little Prince discovers 'five thousand of them, all alike, in one single garden!'

What if there are, in fact, even more gardens like this one?! The horror!

'She would be very much annoyed,' he said to himself, 'if she should see that. ... She would cough most dreadfully, and she would pretend that she was dying, to avoid being laughed at. And I should be obliged to pretend that I was nursing her back to life – for if I did not do that, to humble myself also, she would really allow herself to die ...'

Then he went on with his reflections: 'I thought that I was rich, with a flower that was unique in all the world; and all I had was a common rose ...'

And he lay down in the grass and cried.

Your first love is magical because when you're in love for the first time, you're certain this is your last time too. Furthermore, you're certain that the person you love is the only one in the world with so many graceful and wonderful qualities.

When you fall in love for the second time, it's far less magical, because you know you've felt it all before, and still it ended. How can you be sure this time will be any different? Well, you can't. And when you subsequently love someone else, a third and a fourth and all the rest, you no longer ask such questions because you know that love can end in a split second. This is very sad, but very true too.

Philosopher Alain de Botton, who was born in Zurich and studied philosophy and history at Cambridge, said that we may even meet the love of our life just before we die, or on our very last day on Earth. How will we know that they are the one? Anyone who has ever loved knows that just as love can suddenly appear, so it can end any minute, and a new love suddenly shine upon us. (Incidentally, if you've never read Chekhov's 'The Lady with the Dog', or if you've read it fewer than five times, you must do so the first chance you have.)

***

We left the Little Prince lying on the grass and crying. He can't understand what was so special about his rose that made him love her so. The question to which he is actually trying to find an answer is the ageless one: what is love?

Does love even exist? Perhaps – in a paraphrase of an adage by François de La Rochefoucauld – 'love is like the ghosts in ancient English castles: everyone talks about them, but no one has actually seen them.' Let's give the Little Prince a helping hand.

The Better Half

Plato's *The Symposium* describes a meeting of several very wise men who discuss the eternal question: 'What is love?' Each participant gives a speech, presenting his take on the subject. To me, the prettiest speech of all is delivered by Aristophanes, who was born in Greece in 446 BC (which really was a long time ago: he was a contemporary of Socrates and, in fact, the two even knew but didn't really like each other). He wrote plays for a living, and if you enjoy the theatre you may want to catch his *Lysistrata*, The *Frogs, The Clouds or The Birds*.

Aristophanes opened his speech with a most dramatic announcement. In the distant past, he said, the human race did not comprise two genders, as it does today, but three: there were men attached to men, women attached to women, and men attached to women. These twofold people lived happily and well, but then in hubris they decided to rebel against the gods. Unsurprisingly, Zeus did not appreciate this mutiny, and so he decided to punish them. At first he thought he would just kill them all, but even the mighty Zeus knew that gods exist only when there are people to believe in them, and so he switched to Plan B: he took an axe, cut these twofold people in half, and scattered those halves all over the place.

Now watch this: a story that starts out sounding completely absurd suddenly begins to make perfect sense. I mean, we fall in love because we are not whole. We all miss that mythological other half, and spend our entire lives looking for them. (Incidentally, this myth explains the origins of homosexuality and matches the current view, held by many scientists, according to which sexual tendencies are basically innate.)

What are your chances of finding that other half? Perhaps you're lucky and have already found it? How can you tell?

Aristophanes has the answer, which I shall word as follows. If, by some miraculous chance, Hephaestus the blacksmith god should appear before you and offer to weld you and your current partner so that you are reunited forever, as you were before, and will never part again, then note your own reaction. If you refuse, this is not your real other half. If you hesitate before you accept, this is still not your other half. Only if you leap into the air with joy can you be sure that you've already found your missing half.

But who could meet such a criterion? It's terribly harsh. If you ever want to hang out with your friends instead of spending time with your beloved – even for just one evening – you're out!

How could the Little Prince know the rose was his other half?

It seems that Antoine and Consuelo knew they were two halves of the same entity but were unable to live together for very long nonetheless.

As my grandfather used to say: 'Perfect pairs exist only in shoe stores.'

Dante, Beatrice, Paolo and Francesca

The great Italian poet Dante Alighieri concluded his *Divine Comedy* with the following phrase:

L'amor che muove il sole e l'altre stelle.

I give it to you in Italian because for me Italian is the most beautiful language in the world, and because, very often, you don't have to speak Italian to understand it. Try to guess what this phrase says.

It says: 'The love that moves the sun and the other stars.'

In Yiddish they say: 'Love may not make the world go round, but it gives meaning to its spin.'

All his adult life Dante loved Beatrice. According to *La Vita Nuova* ('The New Life', but isn't the translation redundant?), Dante only met her twice and nine years elapsed between their meetings (which I doubt: they both lived in Florence, and anyone who has spent some time there knows that everyone meets everyone all the time). Dante was married and Beatrice had a husband too (he was a banker, but we forgive her), but still he loved her all his life, even after she died at the age of 26. Describing their second meeting, the great poet relates how he almost died with joy and excitement when she said hello. He said she was *'gentilissima, benedetta, la gloriosa donna della mia mente'*.

I will not translate that. Just read these words out loud and you'll know exactly what Dante felt for her. That feeling, however, helped the poet make an important discovery: he realized that the most romantic love of all is the love that never materializes, and that imagination beats reality every time.

I was moved by the description in *The Divine Comedy's Inferno* (Circle 2, Canto 5) of Dante's meeting with Francesca da Rimini. Here, Francesca tells Dante how she cheated on her husband with his brother Paolo, and how they were both murdered by the husband (all based on historical fact, by the way; Francesca was the daughter of the governor of Ravenna and was Dante's contemporary). While Dante is going to Heaven to unite with Beatrice, he envies Paolo and Francesca whose souls circle around and around in a terrible storm without a moment's rest. Dante gathers that it's better to be with the one you love in Hell than to be in Heaven with someone who does not and will never love you.

While on the subject, here is one of the finest definitions of hell I've ever read:

> What is *hell*? I maintain that it is the suffering of being unable to love.
>
> Fyodor Dostoevsky

Note that hell is not when nobody loves you, but when you're unable to love. A person who loves no one or nothing in this world is indeed in hell.

What Is Love?

'What is love' was the most searched phrase on Google in 2012, when this book was written. This made me very happy. I'd feared that people were no longer looking for love and was thrilled to discover that many do. Furthermore, I was moved by the fact that after millennia of songs and poetry, folktales and philosophies, hieroglyphs and movies, we still don't know for certain what love is. It would appear that the quest for love is a thing that matters.

Simone and Vladimir

As far as split humans go, it's interesting to note that it does sometimes happen that two people who did not know each other and never read each other's works write the very same phrases.

A fine definition of love was phrased by both philosopher Simone Weil and philosopher, mystic and poet Vladimir Solovyov: 'To love someone is to understand he exists.'

We'll be able to understand this statement better after reading my loose translation of a passage from the opening paragraph of Anton Chekhov's 'Rothschild's Violin' (or 'Rothschild's Fiddle' in some translations):

Yakov Ivanov, whose nickname in the street was Bronze, lived in a poor way like a humble peasant, in a little old hut in which there was only one room. In this room he had the coffins he built, a bed for two, a pair of winter shoes, his wife Marfa, a stove, a bench, and other domestic possessions.

Did you notice where Marfa is placed? She's somewhere between the shoes and the stove. She doesn't really exist. She's in Yakov's background, part of the setting (and if you, my reader, have philosophical tendencies, you're welcome to think of Yakov as a solipsist).

To love someone, Vladimir and Simone told us, you need to understand that they exist just like you do, to feel their joy when they are happy, sympathize with their sadness when they are down, and ache with them.

> Love is the difficult realization that something other than oneself is real.
>
> Iris Murdoch

Solovyov wrote a philosophical essay entitled 'The Meaning of Love', in which he presents numerous exciting and far-reaching conclusions. It can be found in certain specialty bookstores, but I must warn you that despite its straightforward title it is not an easy read.

In any event, one of Solovyov's conclusions is that there is only one force that can transcend the pathological egotism we are all afflicted by: the power of love, and even more so, erotic love. To love someone is to want to live with them and no one else for the rest of your life.

> To love someone means that one's willing to grow old besides that person.
>
> Albert Camus

Grow old along with me!
The best is yet to be,
The last of life, for which the first was made:
Our times are in His hand
Who saith 'A whole I planned,
Youth shows but half; trust God: see all, nor be afraid!'

Robert Browning, 'Rabbi ben Ezra'

A Chinese Legend, with Homework

In *Cinema Paradiso*, the Italian film by Giuseppe Tornatore, old Alfredo
tells Salvatore (who was the little boy nicknamed Toto who had just fallen
desperately in love with a girl) an old legend. Below I present you with my
version of that legend, followed by a mental exercise.

The Soldier and the Princess

*One day a simple Chinese soldier happened to see the famously
beautiful Princess Sun-lu as she passed him by in her carriage. That
split second, that single glimpse, struck the soldier dumb. Instantly
he fell head over heels in love with her. But what can a simple soldier
do when he falls in love with a princess? What chance does he have?
Still, when you love someone truly, you do extraordinary things, so the
soldier decided to go to the royal palace, wait for an opportunity to
see the princess again, and confess his great love to her.*

*He went there the very next day and waited by the great stairs
that led to the palace. When he saw the princess taking noble steps
down the stairs, he fell to her feet and told her how he felt. Her
guards immediately attacked him, but just before they beheaded
him the princess said with the faintest of smiles: 'Look, if you want
me so badly, I'll let you be with me – provided that you stand
underneath my window for 100 days and nights. If you do that, I
will be yours.'*

The entire entourage and guards burst out laughing at the clever words of the witty and pretty princess, but the soldier did not laugh. 'That I will do,' he asserted. He went to her garden, positioned himself underneath her window, and stood and stood and stood there. The princess was the first thing on his mind when he woke up in the morning and the last thing he thought of when he fell asleep at night.

He stood there while the sun scorched his face and while heavy rains drenched him and chilled him to the bone. Kind citizens gave him some food and water, and he stood there and did not move for a month, two months, three months. He was totally worn out, but he kept standing, driven by the power of his great love. Night turned into day and day into night, and the soldier stood there, totally devoted. He was still there on the 99th night.

On the 100th day, one night before the princess was about to be his, he looked at her window for the last time, turned around and walked away. No one ever saw or heard of him again.

Homework

Question: Why did the soldier abandon his post one day before completing his mission?

Hint: There may be a few correct answers.

The Secret of the Fox

It was then that the fox appeared. […]

    'Come and play with me,' proposed the Little Prince. 'I am so unhappy.'

    'I cannot play with you,' the fox said. 'I am not tamed.' […]

    'What does that mean – tamed?'

    'It is an act too often neglected,' said the fox. 'It means to establish ties.'

    'To establish ties?'

'Just that,' said the fox. 'To me, you are still nothing more than a little boy who is just like a hundred thousand other little boys. And I have no need of you. And you, on your part, have no need of me. To you, I am nothing more than a fox like a hundred thousand other foxes. But if you tame me, then we shall need each other. To me, you will be unique in all the world. To you, I shall be unique in all the world ...'

'I am beginning to understand,' said the Little Prince. 'There is a flower ... I think that she has tamed me ...'

The Little Prince begins to understand the lesson that the fox has taught him. Note the use of the verb, to tame. Taming is a process that takes a very long time and is based on training, ceremonies and trust. The fox tells the Prince that only when you tame someone do you really know them, and the only people who really know you are those who have tamed you. Now, the Little Prince is beginning to understand that his rose indeed is unique and singular, the only one for him.

The fox sends the Prince to see the roses again, and promises to teach him a great secret on his return. So the Little Prince goes back to the rose garden and understands what the fox has taught him – that his rose is nothing like the other roses. They are all beautiful, of course, but mean nothing to him. He also understands that his rose means nothing to other people, those who don't know her. For the Prince, however, she is the one and only. He has watered her, put her under a glass globe, sheltered her behind the screen, saved her from the caterpillars that wanted to harm her beauty, listened attentively when she was silent, when she grumbled, and when she boasted. He has heard her every complaint, cherished her beauty, made her breakfasts and admired her fragrance. 'She is more important that all the hundreds of you roses … because she is my rose,' the Little Prince tells the garden roses.

When he returns, the fox teaches him another important lesson: 'You become responsible forever for what you have tamed.'

To love someone is to tame him or her, and let them tame you. It's all about the daily rituals of having coffee in the morning, made just the way you like it, and reading together from the same book at night. It's the trust that forms over the years. To love someone is to know the fragrance of their hair every hour of the day, to know how their pillow smells when they go to work before you do. To start whistling the same tune even though you are in different rooms. To want to see the world through their eyes. To know that she is the one and only one for you in the whole world. (You simply must see *Cherry Blossoms*, the most romantic film by Doris Dörrie!)

> Perhaps the feelings that we experience when we are in love represent a normal state. Being in love shows a person who he should be.
>
> Anton Chekhov

The Little Prince loves the rose very much, but as often happens with love he doesn't really understand her, and she (the rose) doesn't understand him at all. When he reaches the deep insight that 'women should be loved without trying to understand them', it is already too late.

And just before the Little Prince goes away, the fox reveals yet another very important and very simple secret to him:

> It is only with the heart that one can see rightly.
> What is essential is invisible to the eye.

5.

In Search of Lost Time

Time is a subject too complicated to understand, and issues associated with time seem to go beyond human perception. St Augustine, in *Confessions*, Book 11, wondered about it too: 'What, then, is time? If no one asks me, I know what it is. If I wish to explain it to him who asks me, I do not know.'

Certainly, whatever happens to us happens in time. There's a time to be born and a time to die, and a time for everything in between these two points in time. Time starts a countdown the moment we're born, constantly flowing toward the Kingdom of Great Darkness beyond.

In a lecture I attended once, the speaker concluded by saying that now we were all 90 minutes closer to death. People in the audience chuckled, but the speaker remarked, quite angrily, that what he said was actually rather sad. The passing of time is a deep and sad truth that no man or woman can change.

Timemory

Time is a notion closely and even immediately associated with the concept of memory. Does memory have meaning if time doesn't exist? What meaning does time have in the absence of memory? We can't speak about time without reference to memory, and vice versa. That's why the title of Proust's masterpiece is translated as both *In Search of Lost Time* and *Remembrance of Things Past*.

All things happen in the realm of time and pass into the field of memory. By the time I play the second bar of a Scarlatti sonata, the first bar has already taken residence in my memory centre. Everything that happens to us immediately turns into memory: the first time I saw snow falling; a bee that stung me in first grade; hugs I've given and received; the birth of my children; the Amalfi Coast on a summer vacation; my parents' 50th wedding anniversary; war experiences; the first time I saw my wife – it's all there, stored in my memory, and nowhere else.

Certain residents of the House of Memory choose to live in the basement. Our minds cannot readily recall each and every experience we've had, and that's not to say we would even like to remember everything. Absolutely not. We all have things we wish we'd never experienced, and still more things we'd love to forget. Still, we can't trust our memory to remember or forget things just because we want to. It appears that our memory is not under our command.

How should we train memory to learn to forget?

Stanisław Lec

Classical physicists tell us that time flows uniformly, but we know that's not true. When we were children, time flowed leisurely. It started picking up speed when we became teenagers and has been accelerating ever since. Heading toward my sixth decade, I've noticed that time travels at scary velocities. Days and even weeks fly by in an instant. That's why Schopenhauer said that from the youth's point of view, life is an endless future, while from the elder's point of view, life is but a brief past.

Time is relative, of course: our happy moments tend to be fleeting, while sorrowful moments sometimes take residence inside our house and, joining several other uninvited guests, refuse to move on. At moments of grace, we can shout: 'Yes! This is great! Hold it right there for a moment.' But time doesn't listen: our call goes unheeded. We can't stop time, not even for a fraction of a second.

Often, with the passing of time, stories or episodes that amused us on first reading take on deeper and sadder meanings when you read them again. Here's one of the saddest:

To Stop a Minute
(Alice and the King are running very fast, when Alice, who is nearly fainting, turns to the King)
'Would you – be good enough,' Alice panted out, after

running a little further, 'to stop a minute – just to get – one's breath again!'

'I'm good enough,' the King said, 'only I'm not strong enough. You see, a minute goes by so fearfully quick. You might as well try to stop a Bandersnatch!'

Lewis Carroll, *Through the Looking-Glass*, Chapter 7

Everyone knows what 'to stop a minute' means in everyday life and in a given context, but the King understands it differently, which is normal, because kings always understand things in ways ordinary people don't. Actually, the King understands things literally.

I must confess that whenever I read this piece, I'm saddened a little because, as we've seen, we know that you really cannot stop a minute, a second, or even a moment. Everything passes, and time is constantly flowing in the wrong direction. Still, things are never that simple, and this time … it can even be a good thing.

Often, under dire and even intolerable circumstances, the fact that time passes encourages us and gives us the strength to cope and deal with issues we couldn't have tackled otherwise. So here's yet another profound truth: time is our greatest enemy and our best friend.

An old Middle Eastern tale sheds some more light on this insight.

There was a king who was wise, generous, and humble. One day he asked his court philosophers to find him the world's wisest sentence – a phrase that would be so wise that it could match every situation, make you happy when you're sad, and sadden you a little when you're too happy. The king wanted it engraved on his ring.

After contemplating this request for three days and nights, the sages returned with the following, very wise and most precise insight:

This too shall pass.

The king had it engraved on his ring.

Time-wasting

As you already know, I tend to take time for myself occasionally in which to do nothing. This is a very important and spiritual thing for me. Quite a few people, however, simply don't get it. They make the bizarre argument: 'Haim, doing nothing is silly. You're wasting time.'

Time, I always reply, is wasting anyway. No matter what I do or don't, time is wasting. That's the very nature of time! Just read this sad dialogue between Alice and the Mad Hatter, which takes place during the Mad Hatter's Tea-Party.

> Alice sighed wearily. 'I think you might do something better with the time,' she said, 'than wasting it in asking riddles that have no answers.'
> 'If you knew Time as well as I do,' said the Hatter, 'you wouldn't talk about wasting it. It's him.'
> 'I don't know what you mean,' said Alice.
> 'Of course you don't!' the Hatter said, tossing his head contemptuously. 'I dare say you never even spoke to Time!'
>
> Lewis Carroll, *Alice in Wonderland*, Chapter 7

> You are really wasting time only when you do things you don't have to and you don't really enjoy doing.
>
> The Shapira–Gefen Principle

British poet Edward Young once wrote in his monumental long poem *Night Thoughts*: 'The bell strikes one. We take no note of time, / But from its loss.' (Night I)

I mean, have you ever heard of anyone who saved time for later? Could the world's most diligent man, who eventually becomes the world's richest man, walk into a Swiss bank later in his life, open a secret safe and withdraw ten years he had saved?

'All my possessions for a moment of time.'

Queen Elizabeth I's famous last words

Time is wasting all the time, but it would be wrong, silly and even cheating a little to say that time is passing. It isn't. Time stays; we pass.

Time goes, you say? Ah, no!
Alas, Time stays, we go ...

Austin Dobson, 'The Paradox of Time' (1886)

Why do people hurry so? What's the rush?

The Russian singer-songwriter Vladimir Vysotsky, who achieved unbelievable fame during his lifetime and had an immense effect on the Russian culture, wrote in one of his songs that 'Everyone is always on time when they come to visit God.'

And, indeed, you have no reason to hurry: no one has ever been late at the Pearly Gates, and no one ever will be.

Quiz: The Meaning of Life

One morning, just as Israeli poet David Avidan wrote (see page 10), I awoke and the morning did not awake in me. The problem was that I only realized this when I was already on my way to teach a psychology class. I hate lecturing when I'm not at my best, so I started thinking up ways to avoid giving a class. Then I noticed it was April Fool's Day, and though I was quite tired I came up with a strategy to salvage the situation elegantly. I decided to give my students a surprise quiz on a really surprising subject. I walked up to the blackboard and wrote in huge letters:

Surprise Quiz
Write a short essay on the Meaning of Life
worth 30% of the final grade.

Now, when students see the magic words 'worth 30 per cent of the final grade', they get so uptight that they can't even remember their own names, let alone the date. Pleased with myself for coming up with such a brilliant way to get through a class effortlessly, I sat back in my chair and relaxed. As I reached for my bag to pull out the newspaper, I noticed that the students were making strange noises. I looked at them and they seemed troubled. Some were shifting impatiently in their chairs, some were tapping their pens on the desk, others stared blankly at the ceiling, trying to find some revelation there. Finally, one student couldn't hold it in anymore. He rose and angrily yelled at me: 'You can't ask us to write about the meaning of life. We didn't prepare for this at all! And it's irrelevant for the course.'

Did you hear that? The student was not prepared for it? He thought the meaning of life was irrelevant! He'd actually never considered the meaning of life. Amazing.

What is even more amazing is the fact that even people who don't have a clue about what they want to do with their lives are still certain they must hurry.

A man who does not know what he wants to do with his life is like an athlete who arrives at the stadium, but forgot what his designated sport is.

Ryūnosuke Akutagawa

Time appears right at the beginning of *Alice in Wonderland*, when we encounter the hurrying and hard-pressed Rabbit who keeps looking at his watch. Whenever I read this passage, I can't help thinking that many of us are like that speeding Rabbit – always in a hurry and always late. It must be part of the nature of rabbits. Eeyore, Pooh's donkey friend, complained that Rabbit (yes, that's another rabbit from another children's story: we have a Rabbit in both *Winnie-the-Pooh* and *Alice in Wonderland*) asked him how he was, but kept running like mad and never waited to hear the answer. That made me think of a new definition for 'friend'. A friend is one who asks 'How are you?' and sticks around to hear the answer. In other words, one who gives you a piece of his time.

> One of the great disadvantages of hurry is that it takes such a long time.
>
> G K Chesterton

This is the time-saving paradox we live through in this day and age. Man has invented all kinds of contraptions – fax machines, microwave ovens, planes, iPhones and so on – that are meant to create more time for us, but the result is just the opposite. Once, when a person wanted a cup of tea, he had to go the forest, cut some wood, chop it down, start a fire, bring a bucket of water from the well, put some in a kettle on top of the fire, and wait for the water to boil – and all the while, he had plenty of time. Today we hit a button and we have boiling water in six seconds while we make a phone call – but where has the time gone?

Once, if we wanted to visit Italy, we took a ship and cruised the ocean for days that were filled entirely with free time. Today we have to catch a taxi to the airport, catch a plane and spend the few flight hours constantly busy – we eat, drink, watch an in-flight movie, do some duty-free shopping, and *boom*: we are there without even a minute to spare. Our attempt to save time has made time vanish completely. People were never as short on time as we are today.

At the Tea-Party scene in *Alice*, time never changes and the clock never moves forward (or backward) because the Mad Hatter has killed Time – literally, physically. In a way, the tea party participants live in a constant present, because only the present exists. In his own way, Pooh too has killed time: he has stopped the clock right at the time to munch on something.

When I'm 64

The Russian revolutionary Leon Trotsky once said that getting old is one of the most surprising things that can happen to a person. Only literary or cartoon characters never grow old. The Little Prince is well over 70; Winnie-the-Pooh recently had his 90th birthday; and Alice deserves our respect for having been around for the past century and a half. The three of them are still full of youthful vigour and will remain so forever (or at least until the Age of Culture ends).

Most of us fear old age, trying to postpone it as much as we can. Wise King Solomon offered a frightening description of old age: while the sun, moon and stars keep shining, the old person's world is swallowed by the Kingdom of Darkness. When we were younger, the sun would reappear after the rain, but for the old folks the clouds never disperse and it rains again as soon as the rain stops. As the old man weeps, tears run from his eyes, but not always down his cheeks: at times his tears run into his soul. His legs wobble, his hands tremble and his spirit is shaking, in fear and terror and awe.

Old Man, Solomon said, you have few teeth and the taste-buds on your tongue are gone too – you've had enough to eat and taste in your long life. Your eyes can't detect shapes and have grown dim – you've seen enough in your lifetime. You have very little to do, but you're always tired – you've done enough this time around. You sleep light because every sound startles you – you've slept enough. Your ears no longer pick up the sounds that used to please you. This world is growing silent and dark. Life is coming to an end and the Kingdom of Terrible Mystery awaits you.

King Solomon's view of old age as 'evil days' is correct, but perhaps so is its opposite: 'old age is a time of joy'. Remember the definition of 'profound truth'? If not, reread 'A Page That Really Matters' (page 47).

I don't know what will happen to me when I'm 64, so I have no opinion on the matter. All I can do is guess

However, many studies have shown that the intuitive view that many of us share, whereby happiness diminishes with age, is wrong. Professor Yang Yang, of the University of Chicago, in an important sociological study of 2008, unequivocally showed that Americans actually grow happier with age. In the introduction to her study, Yang wrote: 'The age effects are strong and indicate increases in happiness over the life course.'

I'm quite certain that some of my readers, who have not lived many days under the sun, are surprised by this finding. 'How can my grandfather be happier than I am? He has no teeth!' 'And what about grandma's osteoporosis? Is this joy?' 'They don't party as much as I do!'

Well, many good things come with age, primarily self-integration and self-esteem. When you're old, you really don't have to do anything you don't want or like to do (such as working under a loathsome boss). You begin to understand what really matters.

My parents' experience taught me how important friends are as you grow older. They have three pairs of very good friends. They meet often, speak on the phone a lot, celebrate their birthdays together, watch movies together, and those who feel better drive those who don't feel as good to hospital when necessary. When I was less aware of the importance of friends, I tried to talk them into moving to a bigger house in a nicer place than theirs, but they refused, using all types of excuses. Today I know the real reason: they simply wanted to stay close to their friends. What good is a big and fancy house if it's filled with loneliness?

Psychological studies on happiness reaffirm the importance of friendships, but they also indicate that we don't make enough efforts to acquire and maintain them.

In any event, I want to tell you about an educational experience I once had. Several years ago I spent a night in the enchanting Italian town of San Gimignano. Most of the tourists who visit the town spend a day there and leave at dusk, but after a nice afternoon nap I went for stroll in the dark and quiet town. It was quite empty. Lots of candles were burning at the tops of the medieval towers. It looked magnificent. Suddenly, I heard loud and happy voices coming from Piazza della Cisterna and started walking toward them. As I turned the corner, I witnessed a human sight that thrilled me almost as much as the beautiful mystery of the town's vistas had just done. There, in the middle of the square, the old men and women of the community had placed a huge table, laden with pizza, plates of bruschetta and dozens of bottles of wine. They ate and drank and chatted loudly, looking like they had no cares in the world.

I told myself, and later my wife, that when I retire I'll go there to sit with those elders and embrace the simple joys of life.

François de La Rochefoucauld said that people are never as happy or as miserable as they think. We can't understand this when we're young. The smallest thing can elevate us and send our soul soaring, while even the tiniest thing might crush us. While old age is rarely accompanied by great festivity, the elderly no longer get too depressed by the small events of life either.

Marcel Proust said that when a man is young, he tries hard to win the heart of the woman he falls in love with, but when he grows older he realizes that knowing he'd won the heart of a woman was enough for him to love her. He believed that as we grow older, we love those who love us. As an admirer of beauty, I know that as I grow older I see beauty in almost every woman.

I suggest that those who haven't yet been convinced that old age is advantageous consider the alternative.

Although, as I've noted, I'm too young to opine about old age, I must share two insights I've had on the matter – one small and one tiny.

First, I believe it's most unfair that old age is so badly timed. We shouldn't have to deal with its hardships when we're old and weary. I truly believe we would all do better if we wrestled with those hardships when we're young and strong.

My second insight is associated with an idea I share with Oscar Wilde. There's one thing about ageing that's worse than all the other problems:

the fact that we do not really grow old. Wilde and I know that the body – that physical entity that hosts and houses my mind and soul – does age and decay, but the dweller therein, the mental me, does not grow old at the same pace, or rather, it stays forever young.

If the mind aged with the body, old age might be a mellow, recreational time for us, but this is often not the case. Living inside this fragile body, our minds and souls cling to their desires and hopes. I know that my desires and dreams today are not much different – neither in the objects of their focus nor in their power – than the dreams and desires I had when I was half my current age.

Writing this, I realize that the above is yet another profound truth, which is why its very opposite is also true. That truth is that I really don't want my soul to grow old along with my body, but I want my body to stay as young as my soul, not age and decay. As sad as it is to see a young soul in an old body, there's nothing sadder than an old soul in a young body.

The Final Curtain

It is said that your life flashes before your eyes just before you die. That is true. It is called Life.

Terry Pratchett

There's an ancient and popular oriental tale (Tolstoy wrote a wonderful version in his *Confessions*) about a wanderer who encountered a horrible beast in the heart of the desert. Trying to escape it, he ran to hide in a dry well he suddenly saw before him. But as soon as he started climbing down, he realized that a dreadful dragon was crouching at the bottom, waiting for his morning snack. Trapped inside the well between the beast and the dragon, and losing his grip on the slippery wall, the wanderer suddenly saw a small branch growing out of the wall. He grasped it with all his might, clenching hard, but his arms grew weaker and weaker. Soon, he realized, he would have to let go and fall to his doom. Suddenly he noticed that two mice, one black and one white, were gnawing at the shrub. Now, all hope was really lost. His fate was sealed by two little mice. Hanging like that, suspended in despair in mid-air, he saw a few drops of dew on that withering branch. He pulled the branch closer to his mouth, stuck out his tongue, and licked the honey droplets. 'Ah,' was his last thought, 'how wonderful is the taste.'

I imagine that my intelligent readers have figured out by now that the white mouse symbolizes day, the black one stands for night, and the dragon is a symbol of our horrific death (or so we imagine death to be). Day follows night, night follows day, and with each cycle we move closer to the dragon. So why not enjoy the wonderful taste of life while we're on our way?

The fact that someone died is not proof that he ever lived.

Stanisław Lec

Spinoza felt that free minds should not dwell on death, only on life. Tolstoy strongly resented that recommendation, and wrote that people who learn to think deeply almost always consider death, consciously or not.

Many people I know are very upset whenever death comes up in conversation; but even if we ignore death, death will not ignore us. Death will come. All the people who walk down the street with you now, everyone who lives in your town, anyone you ever knew, will one day travel to the Kingdom of Eternal Silence.

The countdown started when you were born.

I believe that knowing death is out there can help us live better and wiser, and embrace the things that matter. The German philosopher Martin Heidegger was once asked to give a good tip for a better life. He said that spending plenty of time in cemeteries would be a good idea, because it can help us understand the proximity of death more deeply and live a better life.

Is It Terrible, Ivan?

Tolstoy wrote his wonderful novella *The Death of Ivan Ilyich* when he was almost 60, after surviving strong personal and intellectual turmoil. Vladimir Nabokov believed it was the best story ever written. Speaking to American students, he described this as Tolstoy's most glorious, complete and complex work. Humbly, I agree.

The story has a deep and profound religious layer, though not in the ordinary sense of the word. Of course, it's the story of Ivan Ilyich's life, not death, but his life – just like mine, yours, and everyone else's – takes place in the face of death.

Here's a brief summary of the plot: Ivan Ilyich, a wealthy and respectable man, becomes ill and dies at the age of 45.

In the beginning of the second chapter, Tolstoy tells us that Ivan's life was 'very simple, very ordinary, and thus very terrible'. Ilyich is an ordinary middle-class bourgeois man, spiritually empty, and detached from nature, the Earth and high moral values. A sudden incurable illness arranges a rendezvous for him with the meaning of life and death. His imminent death makes him realize that his entire life has been a lie, that his greatest achievements, legal career and even the big house and the home life he built for his family were all fraudulent. As days go by, his disease torments him greatly. He suffers pain and cries out loud without even being able to relax his vocal chords.

Gerasim, a kind-hearted Cossack, is the only one who understands that Ivan does not need mercy and pity, he needs help. Gerasim's empathy and caring stand in stark contrast to the attitudes of Ivan's other relatives. They may love him in their own way, but they can't help him through this really hard time: they just watch as he withers away. With his kindness and simple, down-to-earth wisdom, Gerasim helps Ivan Ilyich understand what are the right and important things we should do during our brief existence on this Earth. Ivan embraces this wisdom and with its help he even manages to defeat the terrible pain and the fear of death he feels. Though death is right around the corner, Ivan spends his final days on Earth reconciling with everyone and everything, thus bringing closure to his life's story.

'Death is finished,' he said to himself. 'It is no more!'
He drew in a breath, stopped in the midst of a sigh,
stretched out, and died.

End of story

Perhaps one of the greatest tragedies of our lives is that – as the philosopher Søren Kierkegaard put it – life can be understood only in hindsight, but must be lived forward. More often than not, when a person finally understands how to live his life, the Angel of Death appears and tells him: 'Your time is up! That was your life.' How awful!

If there's a lesson to be learned from *The Death of Ivan Ilyich*, it's that we probably should live our lives so that when the time comes to leave this world we don't feel infinite regret and sorrow for a life wasted, spent in vain.

Men may live fools, but fools they cannot die.

Edward Young, *Night Thoughts*, 'Night' IV

Ivan understands how he should have lived just a few days before he dies. How unfair is that? They give introductory classes for almost anything, except for life. You start your life unprepared and go right to the final exam. How nice it would be if we were given a trial run first, and only when we felt ready would we have to take the life given to us and live it, prepared and knowing the things that matter.

I still remember how little I understood when I first read that story of Tolstoy's. I was very young then, living through a period of life in which death rarely ventures into our thoughts, and even when it does, it's just an empty word. In fact, reading about Ilyich at that age is almost a wasted effort. Still, there was one passage in it that I enjoyed even then, though I didn't understand it fully.

When Ilyich realizes he will die, despair takes hold of his heart. Not only is he unable to accept that his death is near and drawing nearer by the minute, he can't understand it either. Then he remembers a classic syllogism that anyone who has ever studied logic knows: 'Socrates is a man, men are mortal, therefore Socrates is mortal' (in the story Tolstoy speaks of Caius, not Socrates).

Ivan Ilyich remembers that syllogism, which always seemed correct to him when applied to Caius, or Socrates, but certainly not as applied to himself. That Caius – Man in the abstract – was mortal, was perfectly correct, but he was not Caius, not an abstract man, but a creature quite, quite separate from all others.

'Caius really was mortal, and so was Socrates, and so are all other mortal humans, and it is right for them to die, but for me, little Vanya, Ivan Ilyich, with all my thoughts and emotions, it's altogether a different matter. It cannot be that I ought to die. That would be too terrible.'

Ivan Ilyich can grasp that all men are mortal but he's unable to wrap his mind around his own death, wondering where he would be when he is no more …

What will you do, God, when I die? […]
Without me what reason have you? […]
It troubles me.

Rainer Maria Rilke

Death: Friend or Foe?

Edward Young, an 18th-century English poet whom Søren Kierkegaard admired, wrote in *Night Thoughts*: 'All men think that all men are mortals but themselves.'

The thing is that it doesn't really matter what we think. The moment of truth will come, sooner or later. In everyone's life there comes a moment in which we grasp and understand that the Grim Reaper will one day pay us a visit. It may be in a few days or in many years, but death will come. That is a singular moment in our lives. From that moment on, we see things differently.

Death is such a huge and overwhelming fact of reality that it consumes everything else. Next to death, life pales. Life is here today, but will be gone tomorrow. Death is near today, will be right here tomorrow, and will stay forever.

Plato believed that people who fear death credit themselves with wisdom they don't have. I mean, everyone fears death and believes it's the worst that can happen to us, but the fact is that no one really knows *death*. For all we know, death could be the best of blessings. A Yiddish saying argues that the afterlife is wonderful: after all, no one ever came back.

According to Plato, Socrates died peacefully when he poisoned himself with hemlock. There are only two options after death, Socrates told his disciples: nothing or life. In the first case, he was headed for a big, dreamless sleep forever. Considering the pleasure we take in a good night's sleep, nothing could be better than an eternal nap (certain Buddhist traditions even maintain that dreamless sleep is the highest state of consciousness). The second option is even more encouraging because, if there's life after death, he'll get to meet Homer and Hesiod, and many other wise and fascinating people that he'd always longed to talk to.

In an old Russian folk tale a very brave soldier (who had helped old ladies cross the street, beat devils at cards, saved the Tsar, and so on) managed to capture Death, and proceeded to tie him up in a large bag. Thus, Death stopped calling, and people stopped dying, and everyone was very happy.

Nevertheless, people kept growing old. Their bodies aged and suffered all kinds of diseases that would not heal. Slowly, they began to realize that Death should be unleashed again to end their misery. They sent delegations, begging the soldier to release his captive. The soldier realized that people were actually suffering because Death was out of commission; and, after thinking about it long and hard, he decided to set Death free to roam.

Death went back to his business and life was back to normal, but only just. Death was so scared of the soldier and his bag that he refused even to pay him a courtesy call. And so, our soldier grew old, tired and ill. He was really fed up with life and, after waiting in vain for a while, he descended to the land of the dead by his own efforts.

The moral of the story is that, frightening as it may be to meet Death, the thought of never meeting him is even scarier.

Death, a Coach for Life

Tolstoy suggested that we adopt death as our mentor – a coach for proper living. Whenever we start wondering what we should do, he said, we simply need to ask ourselves: what would I do (about this or that) if I knew I would die tonight, and no one would ever be the wiser?

If we knew we'd die tonight, would we still be staring at that silly TV game show? Would we be reading yet another article in the economic section of the newspapers? Would we be standing in line to buy something at a discount store? I guess we would do none of those things.

Always expecting death, or the thought that our next few moves will be the last we ever make, could guide us to do the right thing, to live properly, to address ourselves to the things that matter. Death makes life seem more real, sharpening our senses.

I knew a few people whose lives were totally altered once they realized that their death was right around the next corner. After they contracted an incurable disease, they realized how wonderful life is, and how precious is every moment under the sun.

The Tibetan scholar Sogyal Rinpoche suggests:

Looking into death needn't be frightening or morbid. Why not reflect on death when you are really inspired, relaxed, and comfortable – lying in bed, or on vacation, or listening to music that particularly delights you? Why not reflect on it when you are happy, in good health, confident, and full of well-being? Don't you notice that there are particular moments when you are naturally inspired to introspection? Work with them gently, for these are the moments when you can go through a powerful experience, and your whole worldview can change quickly. These are the moments when former beliefs crumble on their own, and you can find yourself being transformed.

Sogyal Rinpoche, *Glimpse of the Day*

Truth is always right there, alongside death. The truth is that we all expect and think about death, whether we admit it or not. The best proof of this is the fact that we all deliberate and think hard before we make a crucial move in our lives. If we knew we would live forever, what would be the point of deliberating? Would I even spend time deciding on my career? Of course not. I'd spend 1,000 years playing the piano in bars and clubs, teach philosophy for the next 1,000 years, spend a few centuries mountaineering, study mathematics for another millennium or so, devote the subsequent millennium to painting, write a few books for another 1,000 years, and I'd still have the whole of eternity ahead of me.

In fact, things are even stranger than that. If we were to think a little about living forever, we'd realize that many philosophers were right when they argued that, given eternal life, most people would actually do nothing at all. After all, why bother solving a mathematical equation today if we can do it tomorrow, or the day after, 100 years from now, or in a billion and a half years?

Ludwig Wittgenstein, one of the greatest philosophers of the 20th century, remarked once that it's wrong to think that if we lived forever, we'd eventually solve all of life's riddles. That's because we'd never even wonder about them. Socrates knew, and many other philosophers agreed, that death is the father of philosophy.

Death gives things value and meaning. It's only because death exists that we choose one thing over another. It's only because we expect to die that our lives can assume an importance, a festive taste, be fruitful and even joyful. Knowing that our time is limited is the only motivator against wasting time – the worst kind of wastefulness. We must work diligently, Tolstoy said, because our work could be terminated at any given moment, and because – in the face of death – there's no point in doing things that are unimportant to us. Knowing that we will die is what motivates us to deal with the things that matter.

6.

On Wisdom and Meaning

You Live Only Twice

Before you go on reading, consider this for a moment. Would you live your life as it has been so far all over again?

Wondering about that myself, I decided to pick the brains of people who have seen many suns rise and set. I chose to ask my father first. He's a Holocaust survivor who has experienced a lot of agony and hardship in his life. I assure you it wasn't easy for me to pose that question to him, but I summoned enough courage and asked whether he would, if he could, live his entire life all over again. Surprisingly, he didn't hesitate and immediately said, 'Yes, I would,' adding that it wasn't even a tough call for him. 'I did not have to think too hard because I experienced quite a few amazing things in my life that are worth repeating despite the horrors I encountered.'

I was a little surprised and very happy. Then, because I don't know enough people of the appropriate research age, I asked my dad to survey his friends and relatives on their willingness to repeat their lives.

He took a few days to conduct his (clearly unscientific) telephone poll. My father's friends were less certain than he was. Some of them didn't want to live their lives again at all, others couldn't provide a conclusive answer even when he asked them to stop telling stories and just answer yes or no.

Eventually it turned out that my father was quite alone in his absolute willingness to repeat his life. Was it his great kindness, his amazing ability to appreciate anything good that came his way, large or small, his real altruism, generosity and total lack of envy that helped him live a life worth repeating?

To Be or Not to Be (the original version)

There are tales of a huge debate between the Hillel and Shamay schools of thought in the first century AD, waged for two and a half years, over which is more convenient for humankind: to be created, or not. After they debated, weighed, calculated and inspected the issue from every angle, the two great sages who led the schools decided that not to be created is better. This, of course, is profound truth – namely, the proposition and its opposite are both true. Not to be created may be better, but life is no less than a miracle.

In any event, these are idle musings for us. After all, we are already here.

To prove that life is a miracle, a word from the German psychologist Erich Fromm:

> Who will tell whether one happy moment of love, or the joy of breathing or walking on a bright morning and smelling the fresh air, is not worth all the suffering and effort which life implies.

Thich Nhat Hanh, a famous Buddhist monk, believed that life is one great miracle:

> The miracle is not to walk on water. The miracle is to walk on the green earth in the present moment, to appreciate the peace and beauty that are available now.

So is life all vanity and suffering, or incomprehensible bliss and endless beauty? You already know that it's both.

Suffering is not the opposite of happiness.

Anonymous

Does the willingness to live a life all over again indicate that it was lived right, respectably and correctly?

Can we learn how to live *while* we live? After all, life is not some college exam – you can't write a draft and then change it, and you certainly don't get a second term.

Which moments of your life so far would you gladly repeat? Which would you rather forget? Try considering events that were up to you and that you don't wish to repeat. Have you learned anything?

The Path of Wisdom

The beginning of wisdom is to desire it.

Solomon ibn Gabirol

All through my teenage and adult life I've often heard the famous adage: wisdom comes with age. I'm still waiting patiently, but as my years accumulate I tend increasingly to doubt that concept. I look at myself, observe my friends, meet with people older than me, and listen to very old folks, but I can't convince myself that with time, people do learn how to better themselves and more wisely live the rest of their lives.

Time isn't such a great teacher after all. Time collects very high tuition fees: it kills all of its students in the end – and that incalculable payment is often utterly wasted.

Some people spend an entire lifetime without learning a thing; others find that experiences teach them accurately and unequivocally. Powerful events open our eyes (if we belong to the latter category) more than months of education – though sometimes we see reality for what it is, while at other times it's distorted.

Clearly, all the grand and lofty ideas have already been spoken and written. Human history carries thousands of versions of wisdom by Eastern and Western poets, prophets, writers, thinkers, scientists and spiritual teachers. Still, a distinction has to be drawn here: knowledge is not the same as wisdom. Knowledge can be handed down from one person to another. Wisdom cannot be transferred. I acquired knowledge from various sources: university lectures, conversations with fascinating people, content-packed Internet sites and, above all, numerous books I've read. They have all added to my sea of knowledge; but wisdom can't be taught.

Knowledge helps you get along in life; while wisdom helps you understand what are the things that matter, and what gives life its meaning.

> Experience is not what happens to you. It's what you do
> with what happens to you.
>
> Aldous Huxley

In my opinion, wisdom is not determined by the amount of knowledge a person acquires throughout his life. There are even people who know so much already that they understand nothing at all. We must beware not to read ourselves to stupidity.

> Wisdom is knowing that you don't know what you don't
> know and that you do know what you know. Stupidity is
> thinking that you know things you don't know or that you
> don't know things you actually do know.
>
> Chinese wisdom

> I am not young enough to know everything.
>
> James M Barrie

Martin Seligman, the father of Positive Psychology, sounds openly sad when he states that 'As a professor I don't like this, but the cerebral virtues – curiosity, love of learning – are less strongly tied to happiness than interpersonal virtues like kindness, gratitude and capacity for love.'

> … that best portion of a good man's life;
> His little, nameless, unremembered acts
> Of kindness and of love.
>
> William Wordsworth, 'Lines Written a Few Miles above Tintern Abbey'

I believe that the level of a person's wisdom is measured by (among other things) the number of happy moments they have collected. Imagine someone who, on his last day on our blue planet, goes over everything he has done in his life. He remembers solving plenty of differential equations, writing three doctorate theses, receiving tenure in two universities. This man has $8.5 million in his bank account. But he was annoyed many times and annoyed others many times also and he can't remember when he was happy … truly happy. He finds it even harder to recall when he made other people happy. He must be very sad.

And so I must ask:

What is the meaning of life? What is the purpose of my life? What should I do with it?

The Russian existentialist Lev Shestov said that life is like a huge wall, and there are two ways to traverse it: either you make yourself very big, develop delusions of grandeur and leap over it; or you make yourself very small, modest and meek, and slip under it. A Central Asian fable says that when a lion attacks you, you can either become a huge warrior and slay it, or make yourself very tiny and hide in one of the lion's teeth cavities.

Jewish sages recommend that the wise maintain two beliefs at all times. According to one, you need truly to believe that the world was created just for you. The other urges that you accept that you are 'nothing but dust and ashes' (Genesis 18:27). The belief that the world was made for you is a profound truth, because its very opposite – 'I am nothing but dust and ashes' – is a truth just as deep. Indeed, people try to get through life either by making giant leaps over that wall or by cautiously crawling under it. Delusions of grandeur coincide with inferiority complexes. We are both manic and depressive. All conflicts inhabit the human soul.

Small wisdom is like water in a glass: clear, transparent, pure.

Great wisdom is like the water in the sea: dark, mysterious, impenetrable.

Rabindranath Tagore

One day the Little Prince met a railway switchman whose job was to help people move from one place to another – some going left and some going right. It appears that all the members of the grown-up tribe are never happy where they are. A friend of mine once said that there's no point in moving from one place to another because wherever you go, you take yourself with you. I don't know where he is now, but he's probably right.

The truth you'll find on top of Mt Everest or in an Indian ashram is your truth, the same truth you brought along with you.

To clarify this, let me quote from Leo Tolstoy's *War and Peace*, the classic novel whose numerous pages contain quite a few philosophical ideas.

'The highest wisdom and truth are like the purest liquid we may wish to imbibe,' he said. 'Can I receive that pure liquid into an impure vessel and judge of its purity? Only by the inner purification of myself can I retain in some degree of purity the liquid I receive.'

There are two types of prayers. People with good intentions pray that the workings of the world change to accommodate them, while the enlightened pray for the power to change themselves. It's critical to realize that those of us who want to fix the world must first try to fix ourselves first.

One man was sitting idly at home when rain started falling. Gradually, the rain grew heavy and then turned into a real storm, with thunder, lightning and heavy rain. Then the man noticed that his roof was leaking. Braving the storm, he put on his coat, stepped out of his house, looked up to the sky, and started directing the clouds and blowing at the wind to go away. 'Rain, rain,' he yelled. 'Go away! Don't fall on my house. And you, clouds, blow away, or move more to the right ... yes, a little more.'

Leo Tolstoy, The Reading Circle

Now, if you ever did what that man had done, kind people in white robes would come to take you away. But wait, Tolstoy said. Isn't it what most people do most of the time? While a storm is raging in their souls, instead of going in to find the leak and fix it – that is, look after their turbulent mind and calm their own spirit – they rush out and try to change their environment.

By the same token, we can see how people are always trying to save the world and change humanity. To be honest, this is a Mission Impossible. However, if each man and woman took care of themselves, mended their homes and pacified their minds, humanity would be saved as a whole. Sages of all cultures knew that.

Most people feel that their inner world is a vast ocean, and they don't have enough courage to dive in, study it and slowly make the necessary changes there. Sooner or later, having failed to find true comfort and peace on the outside, most of us will have to seek refuge inside ourselves. Until then, however, many people choose to save the world instead of saving their souls.

Tolstoy suggested that we stop staging revolutions out on the streets, that we stop changing the world; and that we start being kind to one another. These days, many countries are in turmoil as people take to the streets and seek political reform, social justice, equality, liberty and human rights. Instead, take it easy on the outside, the sages have said, and invest inward. That should make things better.

Gandhi suggested an even bolder tactic. If you want to change the world, 'be the change you want to see in the world'. Gandhi was speaking of the difference between human *being* and human *doing* – believing we should focus on the former.

And maybe, after all, you will reach the sky,
and maybe, after all, you will rejoice in life.
You'll thank it all, and like water you will be,
and you'll be as one with the Mercy Sea.

Kobi Aflalo

Curtain

So what may we conclude from this book? What am I saying, really?

I believe that a good book (and I can only hope this is one of those) is supposed to open our minds to questions, not close and clutter our minds with answers. Often when I read books that offer answers, I feel a little cheated. I believe that each and every one of us must find our own path. Out of respect for my readers, I haven't given you 'Seven Tips for a Better Life', or 'Eight Basic Principles for a Happier Life'.

In the past, psychological studies have mostly focused on the attempt to turn the horrible misery of being a human into 'tolerable suffering', as some early psychologists put it. We must be living in a better time now. People no longer want tolerable suffering at all. They want to be happy and end their adventure on Earth feeling satisfied and complete. And so the best psychologists have rolled up their sleeves and set out to help us.

Today we know about many things that actually improve our quality of life: people with positive thinking live longer; married people are happier; money does wonders for the poor but adds nothing to those who have plenty; believers are happier; education is not a factor in people's happiness; social associations and friendships, on the other hand, significantly add to it. Quite surprisingly, evidence shows that, with the exception of people in their 40s and 50s, most of us are happier as we grow older; it has also been shown that women are both happier and more miserable than men because they have more variance, whatever that means ...

Now, what are we to do with this multitude of information that's mostly based on statistical analyses? Statistics, we all know, is a science that can tell us the probability of chance outcomes when we flip a coin 1,000 times, but is of no use to us when we get to flip it only once. Studies are valid for large groups, but there's almost nothing we can deduce from them when considering a single person.

Remembering those insights and keeping them in the back of our minds is all well and good, but if we seek meaning and wisdom we shall have to make our own individual journey to find them. At best, these academic findings can serve as road signs along the way.

My Way (I Did It)

Instead of giving you tips – which is the smallest currency conceivable and thus, for the most part, useless – I'll tell you about my journey to the valley of big questions. I was greatly influenced by King Solomon, the wisest of all men, and though he lived three millennia before me, some of his recommendations served to light my way and provide instructions for living life. Here's what I've learned so far:

Do Not Give Up on Life's Pleasures

Whatever your hand finds to do, do it with all your might.

Ecclesiastes 9:10

The wise king suggests that we try our hand at everything we can. This idea came at least two millennia before Nietzsche suggested that·it's better to regret things we did than to be sorry for things we didn't do, given that sorrow for the latter is infinite.

So, enjoy yourself. Love a man, woman or child. Go see the Dolomites. Kiss in the rain. Write your memoirs. Read a few philosophy books or, better still, revisit some children's books. Swim with abandon. Insist. Fight. Forgive. Sing in the shower. Pause to observe the cherry blossom. Study maths. Learn a foreign language. Get upset. Get angry. Get sad. Be happy. Admire. Wonder. Pray. Whatever your hand finds to do, do it with all your might.

The light is sweet, and it is good for the eyes to see the sun.

Ecclesiastes 11:7

I can actually envision King Solomon sitting on his huge throne, on a mountain of embroidered cushions, in the splendid garden of his enormous palace. It's early in the morning and the sun, rising behind the Temple, lights up the tall palm trees and dances on the hair of dozens of beautiful women who sit next to him or play beneath his feet. The king looks around, picks up a scroll and a feather, and writes: 'Vanity of vanities. All is vanity.' All shall pass into nothing.

Solomon is thrilled by the beauty that fills his eyes. Life is great, light is sweet, and it's good to see the sun and all the things it shines on. But why does it all have to end? The king loves life passionately and hates it at the same time.

> To think in terms of either pessimism or optimism over-simplifies the truth. The problem is to see reality as it is.
>
> Thich Nhat Hanh

Acquire a Friend

> Two are better than one because they have a good return for their labour. For if either of them falls, the one will lift up his companion. But woe to the one who falls when there is not another to lift him up.
>
> Ecclesiastes 4:9–10

Get Busy – Live a Life of Labour

> The sleep of the working man is pleasant, whether he eats little or much; but the full stomach of the rich man does not allow him to sleep.
>
> Ecclesiastes 5:12

Through indolence the rafters sag, and through slackness
the house leaks.

Ecclesiastes 10:18

Try to Be Happy

Indeed, if a man should live many years, let him rejoice in
them all, and let him remember the days of darkness, for
they will be many. Everything that is to come will be futility.

Ecclesiastes 11:8

Ecclesiastes (Solomon) knew that the ability to be happy is God-given.
Today's scientists call this 'good genetic disposition'. The name doesn't
really matter. Even though the ability to rise on a dark and rainy morning
with a smile on your face is actually genetic, it's important that we
remember: it is so only in part. A wise man can try to learn how to be
happy and uproot anger from his heart.

Don't Long for the Past

Do not say, 'Why is it that the former days were better than
these?' For it is not from wisdom that you ask about this.

Ecclesiastes 7:10

King Solomon suggests that we avoid nostalgia. Longing for bygone years is
neither wise nor beneficial. It's stupid to think that things were better once.
My personal experience has taught me that, quite often, I miss the past
because I'm not too happy with my present state. People usually remember
an idyllic past that's actually far removed from what really happened.

And here's one of my favourite recommendations:

Don't Be Righteous (or Right) All the Time

Do not be excessively righteous and do not be overly
wise. Why should you ruin yourself? Do not be excessively

wicked and do not be a fool. Why should you die before your time? It is good that you grasp one thing and also not let go of the other; for the one who fears God comes forth with both of them.

Ecclesiastes 7:16–18

Don't you be so (self-)righteous now! Everyone knows that everyone's a sinner.

I could never stand the hypocrites who pretended to be angels that have just descended from Heaven. I've never believed people who say they always do good and nothing but good. The worst versions of this type of person are the 'preachers' – those who lecture you about being moral toward others, stressing that they are, of course, spotless in that regard.

Good and bad struggle with each other in everyone's heart. All of us have thoughts we're ashamed of. All of us have done some things we're not too proud of. The key word is moderation. There really is no black and white, only shades of grey.

Prince Antoine

Ever since I turned 40, I've made a point of re-reading chapters and passages of *The Little Prince*. I find it a poetic and philosophical book that gently whispers great truths. On days when sadness fills my heart and I start thinking that perhaps nothing we do under the sun has meaning, that it's all vanity of vanities, I can hear Antoine de Saint-Exupéry explaining: if there's any meaning to the things we do, it's found in the simple yet most important things, the *things that matter*: the ability to remain a child a little while longer; the ability to be someone's friend; and, above all, the ability to love a single flower.

The Natural Way and the Path of Grace

I have spent hours reading and contemplating two philosophers whom

I love very much, the Danish philosopher Søren Kierkegaard and the French philosopher Simone Weil. I owe them and the American film director Terrence Malick for the thoughts that follow.

There are two roads to take on the path of life. One is the natural way, in which we follow our natural inclinations, and this is not the desirable way to go. People who go that way are always busy comparing themselves with others, and their hearts are filled with envy. They tend to get mad easily – either at other people or at their own sad realities. They seek respect and fame and fortune, and are attracted to dark passions. The natural way is the way of a rock rolling downhill. It requires no effort.

The path of grace is different. People who choose it accept (or at least try to accept) everyone and everything as they are, with great love and compassion. Every aspect of Creation thrills them. They feel and express endless gratitude for their very existence. They neither judge nor patronize anyone. They neither envy others nor seek honour for themselves. Choosing the path of grace is hard, and walking it is even harder. In fact, it's nearly impossible. Sometimes, just knowing that the path of grace exists fills my heart with great joy, even though I am not yet on that path.

That great thinker Søren Kierkegaard maintained that once a person finds the path of grace in his heart and fully enters the realm of love, the world – however imperfect it may be – becomes rich and beautiful, consisting entirely of opportunities for love. Eternity, he believed, will ask me (and you, and you) only one question: have you lived your life in despair or in love? Despair is a sign of a life lived wrongly. Despair is vanity turned upside down. Love is the way.

Taking the path of grace is like trying to roll a particularly heavy rock up a hill. If you stop paying attention, if you get distracted, even for a split second, the rock will immediately start rolling back down. The natural inclination to take the natural path lurks at every corner at all times. Simone Weil believed that though we rarely do evil things, we often have evil thoughts – and they are the kind of thoughts that take a person where he or she does not want to go.

Anyone who takes the path of grace acquires a real truth for themselves. It's an authentic truth, one they may be willing to die for, but certainly want to live with. Truth must be personal. Or, as Kierkegaard put it: 'The crucial thing is to find a truth that is true for me.'

Between the natural way and the path of grace there's a deep abyss. It's in that gap that we live our lives as a giant struggle between good and evil, Satan and God, despair and love. Whenever despair wins, it's the natural way. Whenever love wins, it is a moment of grace. When love is victorious and defeats despair completely, you've reached the path of grace.

So, two roads diverge in life. The choice is ours, and the things that matter to us will light our way.

Bon Voyage.

Haim Shapira

Happiness: A Summary

A. Happiness is the meaning and purpose of life.

B. Different people have different perceptions of happiness. Some of us must go bungee jumping to trigger our rush of joy, while others will find their bliss staying at home; some of us are happy in a concert hall listening to classical music, while the cacophony of children in a playground could be music to the ears of others; some people find elation when they solve a complicated equation, while for others a cancelled maths class is a happy childhood memory. And so on.

C. There are no universal rules for being happy – the path leading to happiness is very narrow, with room for one person alone.

D. Knowledge is a must when you try to solve a differential equation or prepare a truffle pie, but it's quite useless when you seek happiness. All smokers know that smoking is unhealthy; and what do they do with this knowledge?

E. As strange as it may sound, we usually don't know what will make us happy.

F. When you awake in the morning and feel no morning awake in you, the best thing to do is to get right back between the sheets, for just two more hours … or five, or ten.

G. It isn't really hard to do nothing. Many of us can. The hard part is doing nothing without feeling guilty about it.

H. It's really important to know when to act and when to let things just happen.

I. Anger is punishing yourself for your own stupidity.

J. It's a scientific fact that people who are easily irritated and lose their tempers live shorter lives; so try to make a habit of getting angry only when there's a chance that your rage will change something.

K. Anyone who has lived on this planet long enough knows that pessimism is the natural way to think. It requires no effort, like a rock rolling downhill. It's much harder to push the rock up the hill; that is, to think positively.

L. Ordinary people who live their lives peacefully, whose days gently resemble each other, may one day just stop and wonder: why do they do the things they do, and have been doing for so many years?

M. It's much easier to choose to be a good person than to think good thoughts.

N. The more flaws one sees in others, the more flaws one possesses.

O. We shouldn't delude ourselves into believing that we can easily discard unwanted emotions. This idea is hubris par excellence: not everything follows our own will and desire.

P. It's always a good idea to take a break, rest a little, do nothing for an hour or two, and munch on a little something.

Q. Modesty and humility are two different things: modesty is often a kind of pride in disguise, while true humility is the rarest and one of the most beautiful of human qualities.

R. Delusions of grandeur and an inferiority complex often cohabit in the psyche of the same person.

S. A love that's based on 'because' or 'thanks to' won't last long if that love doesn't include 'despite of' too.

T. First love is magical because only when you're in love for the first time are you certain this is your last time too.

U. Time is relative of course: our happy moments tend to be fleeting, while sorrowful moments sometimes take residence inside our house and refuse to move on.

V. Many people are very upset whenever death comes up in conversation; but even if we ignore death, death won't ignore us. All the people who walk down the street with you now, everyone who lives in your town, everyone you ever knew, will one day travel to the Kingdom of Eternal Silence.

W. Knowing that death is out there can help us live better and wiser lives, and embrace the things that really matter. We should live our lives so that, when the time comes to leave this world, we don't feel infinite regret and sorrow for a life wasted, spent in vain.

X. So is life all vanity and suffering, or incomprehensible bliss and endless beauty? We all know that it's both.

Y. Good and bad struggle with each other in everyone's heart. All of us have thoughts we're ashamed of. All of us have done some things we're not too proud of. There really is no black and white, only shades of grey.

Z. Love a man, woman or child. Go see the Dolomites. Kiss in the rain. Write your memoirs. Read a few philosophy books or, better still, revisit some children's books. Swim with abandon. Insist. Fight. Sing in the shower. Pause to observe the cherry blossom. Learn a foreign language. Get upset. Get angry. Forgive. Get sad. Be happy. Admire. Wonder. Pray.

It's better to regret things we did than be sorry for things we didn't do, given that sorrow for the latter is infinite.

Notes

Chapter 1 Happiness Matters

p7   The imaginary Heine quote is based on his famous saying: 'All I
         really want is enough to live on, a little house in the country ... and
         a tree in the garden with seven of my enemies hanging in it.'

p23   The quotation beginning 'When we talk to God ...' is from Jane
         Wagner, *In Search for Signs of Intelligent Life in the Universe* (stage
         show), 1986, performed by Lily Tomlin.

p25   The quotation from Joe Bousquet is to be found in Gilles Deleuze,
         The Logic of Sense, trans. Mark Lester, University of Columbia
         Press, 1993 (first published 1969).

p26   *Fight Club* is a 1999 film directed by David Fincher with a
         screenplay by Jim Uhls. It is based on the novel of the same title
         by Chuck Palahniuk.

p31   Colin Wilson's actual sentence about pessimism is: 'It is to be
         suspected that literary pessimism is usually an expression
         of intellectual laziness.' It comes from his book *The Strength to
         Dream: Literature and the Imagination*, Houghton Mifflin (Boston,
         Mass.) and Victor Gollancz (London), 1962.

Chapter 2 Emotions and Desires

p87   The 1971 musical comedy-drama movie *Fiddler on the Roof* was
         produced and directed by Norman Jewison. It is an adaptation
         of a 1964 Broadway musical with music by Jerry Bock, lyrics by
         Sheldon Harnick and book by Joseph Stein, based on stories
         by Sholem Aleichem (the pen name of Solomon Naumovich
         Rabinovich) featuring Tevye the Dairyman.

p88   The 2010 movie *Wall Street: Money Never Sleeps* was directed by
         Oliver Stone and written by Allan Loeb and Stephen Schiff.

Chapter 3 Imagination

p99   This poem is from Lea Goldberg's *Poems Vol 2,* translated by
        Baruch Gefen, Sifriat Poalim (Tel Aviv), 1973.

Chapter 4 On Love, Briefly; or, What the Fox Knows

p119   The two quotations from Tolstoy's *Anna Karenina* are taken from an
        English rendition to be found online at http://tolstoy.thefreelibrary.
        com/anna-karenina.

Chapter 5 In Search of Lost Time

p135   The 'Shapira–Gefen principle' is a principle invented by the
        author and his translator, Baruch Gefen.

p140   The study by Professor Yang Yang is published in *Social
        Inequalities in Happiness in the United States, 1972 to 2004: An
        Age-Period-Cohort Analysis, American Sociological Review,* 73(2),
        204–26.

Chapter 6 On Wisdom and Meaning

p159   The passage quoted from Leo Tolstoy's *War and Peace* is from
        the 1922 translation by Louise and Aylmer Maude, now available
        from CreateSpace Independent Publishing Platform (2014) and
        as a Kindle ebook.

Bibliography

The following is not a typical bibliography. It is a tiny list of some of my favourite books that influenced the writing of *Happiness and Other Small Things of Absolute Importance*.

Agnon S Y, *Only Yesterday*, trans. Barbara Harshav, Princeton University Press, New Jersey, 2002 (first published in Hebrew 1945)

Aurelius, Marcus, *Meditations*, trans. Martin Hammond, intro. Diskin Clay, Penguin Classics, London, 2006 (first published in Latin 180 AD)

Ben-Shahar, Tal, *Choose the Life You Want: The Way to Lasting Happiness Moment by Moment*, The Experiment, New York, paperback edn 2014 (first published 2009)

Botton, Alain de, *The Consolations of Philosophy*, Penguin, London, new edn 2001 (first published 2000)

Camus, Albert, *The Myth of Sisyphus*, trans. Justin O'Brien, intro. James Wood, Penguin, London, 2000 (first published in French 1942)

Carroll, Lewis, *The Annotated Alice: The Definitive Edition*, illustr. John Tenniel, ed. Martin Gardner, W W Norton, New York, 1991 (first published 1960)

Carroll, Lewis, *The Complete Works of Lewis Carroll*, illustr. John Tenniel, leatherbound edn, Barnes & Noble, New York, 2005 (first published 1898)

Dick, Philip K, *Do Androids Dream of Electric Sheep?* (filmed as Blade Runner), intro. Roger Zelazny, Del Rey/Ballantine Books, New York, 1996 (first published 1968)

Dostoyevsky, Fyodor, *Notes from the Underground and The Gambler*, trans. Jane Kentish, intro. Malcolm V Jones (Oxford World's Classics), Oxford University Press, Oxford (UK) and New York, 2001

Epicurus, *The Essential Epicurus*, trans. Eugene O'Connor, ed. Robert M Baird and Stuart E Rosenbaum, Prometheus Books, Amherst, NY, 1993

Heschel, Abraham Joshua, *God in Search of Man: A Philosophy of Judaism*, Farrar, Straus & Giroux, New York, 1976 (first published 1955)

Huxley, Aldous, *The Perennial Philosophy*, Harper Perennial Modern Classics, 2004 (first published 1944)

Kierkegaard, Søren, *Works of Love* ('Kierkegaard's Writings', vol. 16), ed. Howard Vincent Hong and Edna Hatlestad Hong, Princeton University Press, New Jersey, 1998 (first published in Danish 1847)

Lem, Stanisław, *Solaris*, trans. Joanna Kilmartin and Steve Cox, Harcourt, San Diego, 2002 (first published 1961)

Milne, A A, *The Complete Tales of Winnie-the-Pooh*, Dutton Books for Young Readers, Boston, Mass., 1996

Nietzsche, Friedrich, *Human, All Too Human*, trans. R J Hollingdale, Cambridge University Press (UK), 1996 (first published in German 1878)

Pascal, Blaise, *Pensées*, trans. A J Krailsheimer, Penguin Classics, London, 1995 (first published in French 1669)

Sogyal Rinpoche, *The Tibetan Book of Living and Dying*, HarperOne, New York, 2012 (first published 1992)

Rochefoucauld, François de La, Maxims, intro. Leonard Tancock, Penguin Classics, Harmondsworth (UK), 1982 (first published in French 1665)

Saint-Exupéry, Antoine de, *The Little Prince*, trans. Richard Howard, Harcourt, San Diego, 2000 (first published in French 1943)

Schopenhauer, Arthur, *Essays and Aphorisms*, trans. R J Hollingdale, Penguin Classics, Harmondsworth (UK), 1973 (first published 1851)

Szymborska, Wisława, *Nonrequired Reading*, with Clare Cavanagh, Houghton Mifflin Harcourt, Boston, Mass., 2002 (first published in Polish 1973)

Tolstoy, Leo, *How Much Land Does a Man Need? and Other Stories*, trans. Ronald Wilks, intro. A N Wilson, Penguin Classics, London, 1994 (first published in Russian 1885)

Tolstoy, Leo, *The Death of Ivan Ilych*, trans. Aylmer Maude, Waking Lion Press, West Valley City, Utah, 2006 (first published in Russian 1886)

Whitman, Walt, *Leaves of Grass*, Simon & Schuster, New York, 2006 (first published 1855)

Weil, Simone, *Gravity and Grace*, Routledge, London, 2002 (first published in French 1947)

Wittgenstein, Ludwig, *Philosophical Investigations*, trans. G E M Anscombe, 50th Anniversary Commemorative Edition, Blackwell, Oxford, 2001 (first published in German 1953)